Unreal Engine 4 AI Programming Essentials

Create responsive and intelligent game AI using
Blueprints in Unreal Engine 4

Peter L. Newton

Jie Feng

PUBLISHING

BIRMINGHAM - MUMBAI

Unreal Engine 4 AI Programming Essentials

First published: March 2016

Production reference: 1110316

Published by Packt Publishing Ltd.
Livery Place
35 Livery Street
Birmingham B3 2PB, UK.

ISBN 978-1-78439-312-0

www.packtpub.com

Credits

Authors
Peter L. Newton
Jie Feng

Reviewer
Hamad A. Al-Hasan

Commissioning Editor
Edward Bowkett

Acquisition Editor
Larissa Pinto

Content Development Editor
Merint Thomas Mathew

Technical Editor
Dhiraj Chandanshive

Copy Editor
Shruti Iyer

Project Coordinator
Judie Jose

Proofreader
Safis Editing

Indexer
Tejal Daruwale Soni

Production Coordinator
Aparna Bhagat

Cover Work
Aparna Bhagat

About the Authors

Peter L. Newton gravitated toward computers at a young age. As his appetite for technology grew, web applications were his first exploration into development. The excitement of programming is what kept Peter diving further into different software designs and programming patterns. He is a self-taught programmer who has spent countless hours in reverse engineering assembly and arm instruction executables just for the joy of learning. Peter has several years of experience as a web developer, software developer, database architect, and hardware technician. His recent years were dedicated to the Virtual Reality/Gaming industry experience, working with such companies as Create, Sony Pictures, and the developers of Unreal Engine 4, Epic Games.

Peter's most recent VR project was *Can You Walk The Walk?*, which won Digital Hollywood's "Best In Virtual Reality Based on a Cinematic or Television Experience" award.

Thank you, readers, for your continued support in my AI adventures! I've created many tutorials, and because of your overwhelming response, I was reached out to by Epic Games, who requested my services as AI programmer. I've also made quite a few friends, such as Micheal Allar, Chance Ivey, Nick Whiting, Alexander Paschall, Yoeri, Jan, Pete, and many I'm likely to forget, and this is just to name a few. It has been an amazing few years! Living Epic!

Jie Feng is originally from Jiaxing, China. He is currently a PhD candidate at Columbia University, specializing in machine learning and computer vision. He has conducted research on problems ranging from detecting and recognizing objects in images and retrieving similar images from large-scale databases to understanding human behavior in videos. Jie's work has been published at top international conferences, and he has been granted a U.S. patent. He is also a software designer and developer and has worked at Microsoft, Amazon, and Adobe. Jie is passionate about applying Artificial Intelligence to real-world problems. His project using Microsoft Kinect to analyze motion for fitness has won People's Choice Award at Innovative Health Tech NYC competition, 2013. Jie is currently working on a fashion discovery product named EyeStyle.

Video games are the very thing that motivated him to study computer science. His favorite genre is action adventure. Titles including Resident Evil, Tomb Raider, and Uncharted inspire him in innovative thinking. This book is a unique experience for Jie to put his knowledge on Artificial Intelligence to game design and examine the potential of creating intelligent characters using Unreal Engine 4.

I would like to thank my parents for their unconditional love and support for my work and every decision I have made in my life. I feel lucky to have many talented people as my friends and colleagues, both in China and the U.S.. Last but not least, I want to express my appreciation to all game designers and developers out there for creating the fantasy world that inspires people and enriches their lives.

About the Reviewer

Hamad A. Al Hasan has a passion for games and game development and it has taken him far from the shores of Bahrain, where he graduated from Bahrain University in computer science. After working for a couple of years as software engineer, he jumped across the sea and the ocean to work as a gameplay programmer for Action Mobile Games in USA on their Infected Wars title. Hamad developed a passion for Unreal Engine, which then took him to Serbia at Digital Arrow and to Saudi Arabia as a consultant for Semanoor, the publisher of Trails of Ibn Battuta. After this, he worked as technical director for Empire Studios, a local game studio, in which he played a key role in establishing the studio as well as overseeing all the technical aspects of an unannounced mobile game.

Since 2010, Hamad has worked on a variety of systems, be it about player movements, camera and controls, Artificial Intelligence, networking and replication, weapons, different customizations, HUD, or Menus. He is equally familiar with Unreal Editor and its tools and has also developed a strong expertise in material and shader creation. Back in Bahrain, Hamad works on his own projects while continuing his freelance work.

You can contact him at http://www.alhasanstudio.com/.

www.PacktPub.com

eBooks, discount offers, and more

Did you know that Packt offers eBook versions of every book published, with PDF and ePub files available? You can upgrade to the eBook version at www.PacktPub.com and as a print book customer, you are entitled to a discount on the eBook copy. Get in touch with us at customercare@packtpub.com for more details.

At www.PacktPub.com, you can also read a collection of free technical articles, sign up for a range of free newsletters and receive exclusive discounts and offers on Packt books and eBooks.

https://www2.packtpub.com/books/subscription/packtlib

Do you need instant solutions to your IT questions? PacktLib is Packt's online digital book library. Here, you can search, access, and read Packt's entire library of books.

Why subscribe?

- Fully searchable across every book published by Packt
- Copy and paste, print, and bookmark content
- On demand and accessible via a web browser

Table of Contents

Preface

Artificial Intelligence (**AI**) is an essential part of any game. It makes the virtual world we create more immersive and fun to play in. Game AI is different from the general scientific AI that we know; it is more targeted to solve key problems in game design, including navigation, which is how a **nonplayer character** (**NPC**) should move from one point to another and avoid obstacles; decision making, which is how to perform certain actions based on different situations; and environment sensing, which is the ability to understand what exists in the environment and what its status is. These techniques make it possible to create a dynamic and realistic gameplay so that the players will be more engaged in the world that is created for them.

Game AI is complicated and brings a lot of challenges if you want to develop on your own. Unreal Engine 4 is a powerful game engine that provides rich functionalities to create cross-platform 3D and 2D games. It is well known for its advanced graphics and highly customizable components. Now, it is free to use and open source, which makes it one of the most popular game engines out there. Unreal Engine 4 comes with a complete suite of tools for game AI, including NavMesh, Behavior Trees, and Environment Query System. With these tools in hand, it is much easier to bring AI to your games. For game designers, you can even use a visual scripting tool called Blueprints to build your game logic, including AI, by just connecting nodes and without even writing a single line of code.

This book is our effort to introduce these wonderful tools in Unreal Engine 4 to build game AI to game creators who are interested in making their virtual world more interesting. It will cover all the components we have mentioned and show you how to use each tool to build different character behaviors and combine them to create more complex scenes.

We can't wait to see what you will create!

What this book covers

Chapter 1, Introduction to Game AI?, introduces the basic idea of AI and how it directly affects and enhances the gaming experience. You will learn the differences between the traditional and game-specific goals of AI.

Chapter 2, Creating Basic AI, helps you create your first AI step by step and talks about the techniques we will demonstrate along the way. We will dive right into Unreal Engine 4, using the bare components needed to create a single state with random movement for your AI.

Chapter 3, Adding Randomness and Probability, teaches you how to create random and probability techniques that can be used to add randomness, chance, and character to AI, which will make the game unpredictable and more interesting. We will cover how these are used within Unreal Engine 4.

Chapter 4, Introducing Movement, explains how to introduce movement to our AI characters within Unreal Engine 4. Path Finding will be used to allow our character to intelligently navigate within a level.

Chapter 5, Giving AI Choices, explains how to introduce autonomous behavior to our characters using Behavior Trees. Behavior Trees are a methodology that allows you to construct your AI logic visually in a tree structure and can be reused in different characters.

Chapter 6, How Does Our AI Sense?, explains how to use the different components available within Unreal Engine 4 to enable our AI to sense other AI and the pawns we will place within the world.

Chapter 7, More Advanced Movement, focuses on flocking and more advanced path-following behaviors. Flocking allows us to create group behaviors for several AI characters.

Chapter 8, Creating Patrol, Chase, and Attack AI, combines some of the components we used in the previous chapters, including AI Sense and Movement, to have our AI character navigate. Then, we will apply randomness to the time that the AI character will spend chasing after the characters it detects.

Chapter 9, What Have We Learned?, briefly glances over the previous chapters. We will also talk about additional examples of what we can achieve with these combined lessons.

What you need for this book

All you need is Unreal Engine 4.7.0, and you can download it from `https://www.unrealengine.com`.

Who this book is for

This book is for programmers and artists who want to expand their knowledge of game AI in relation to Unreal Engine 4. It is recommended that you have some experience of exploring Unreal Engine 4 prior to this book because we will jump straight into game AI.

Conventions

In this book, you will find a number of text styles that distinguish between different kinds of information. Here are some examples of these styles and an explanation of their meaning.

Code words in text, database table names, folder names, filenames, file extensions, pathnames, dummy URLs, user input, and Twitter handles are shown as follows: "Now, place a comment around this and name it `Chase Hero`."

New terms and **important words** are shown in bold. Words that you see on the screen, for example, in menus or dialog boxes, appear in the text like this: "If you're in Unreal Engine and you navigate to the **Modes** panel under **Volumes**, you'll see **NavMeshBoundsVolume**."

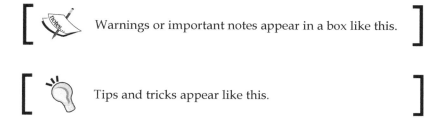

Warnings or important notes appear in a box like this.

Tips and tricks appear like this.

Reader feedback

Feedback from our readers is always welcome. Let us know what you think about this book—what you liked or disliked. Reader feedback is important for us as it helps us develop titles that you will really get the most out of.

To send us general feedback, simply e-mail feedback@packtpub.com, and mention the book's title in the subject of your message.

If there is a topic that you have expertise in and you are interested in either writing or contributing to a book, see our author guide at www.packtpub.com/authors.

Customer support

Now that you are the proud owner of a Packt book, we have a number of things to help you to get the most from your purchase.

Downloading the example code

You can download the example code files for this book from your account at http://www.packtpub.com. If you purchased this book elsewhere, you can visit http://www.packtpub.com/support and register to have the files e-mailed directly to you.

You can download the code files by following these steps:

1. Log in or register to our website using your e-mail address and password.
2. Hover the mouse pointer on the **SUPPORT** tab at the top.
3. Click on **Code Downloads & Errata**.
4. Enter the name of the book in the **Search** box.
5. Select the book for which you're looking to download the code files.
6. Choose from the drop-down menu where you purchased this book from.
7. Click on **Code Download**.

Once the file is downloaded, please make sure that you unzip or extract the folder using the latest version of:

- WinRAR / 7-Zip for Windows
- Zipeg / iZip / UnRarX for Mac
- 7-Zip / PeaZip for Linux

Downloading the color images of this book

We also provide you with a PDF file that has color images of the screenshots/ diagrams used in this book. The color images will help you better understand the changes in the output. You can download this file from `http://www.packtpub. com/sites/default/files/downloads/ LearningUnrealEngineAIProgramming_ ColorImages.pdf`.

Errata

Although we have taken every care to ensure the accuracy of our content, mistakes do happen. If you find a mistake in one of our books—maybe a mistake in the text or the code—we would be grateful if you could report this to us. By doing so, you can save other readers from frustration and help us improve subsequent versions of this book. If you find any errata, please report them by visiting `http://www.packtpub. com/submit-errata`, selecting your book, clicking on the **Errata Submission Form** link, and entering the details of your errata. Once your errata are verified, your submission will be accepted and the errata will be uploaded to our website or added to any list of existing errata under the Errata section of that title.

To view the previously submitted errata, go to `https://www.packtpub.com/books/ content/support` and enter the name of the book in the search field. The required information will appear under the **Errata** section.

Piracy

Piracy of copyrighted material on the Internet is an ongoing problem across all media. At Packt, we take the protection of our copyright and licenses very seriously. If you come across any illegal copies of our works in any form on the Internet, please provide us with the location address or website name immediately so that we can pursue a remedy.

Please contact us at `copyright@packtpub.com` with a link to the suspected pirated material.

We appreciate your help in protecting our authors and our ability to bring you valuable content.

Questions

If you have a problem with any aspect of this book, you can contact us at `questions@packtpub.com`, and we will do our best to address the problem.

1
Introduction to Game AI

This chapter will introduce the basic idea of **Artificial Intelligence (AI)** and how it directly affects and enhances the gaming experience. You will learn the differences between the traditional and also the game-specific goals of AI. We will introduce various techniques used in game AI, including navigation, Behavior Tree, sensor systems, and so on. You will learn in brief which tools we utilize for AI within Unreal Engine 4's editor. After this chapter, readers will gain a basic understanding of how AI can be applied to game development for a better gaming experience. The AI techniques that we will briefly cover here will be taught in the subsequent chapters.

Game Artificial Intelligence

When you first think of Artificial Intelligence, robots immediately come to mind. AI is derived from the idea of intelligence that helps living creatures make decisions. We take inputs, context, and our personal reasoning to decide on the actions we will perform. In AI, we try to virtually replicate this process to create systems that can have autonomous behavior. Assuming you have a fairly extensive gaming history, you would know that game AI is generally not smarter than some older games where your enemy may get stuck in a corner and fail to get out. Game AI now is by no means comparable to the general AI in scientific research. Game AI is designed to work in a well-controlled, predicable virtual world. It mainly consists of hardcoded rules to allow game actors to make proper actions corresponding to different situations. Game AI is meant to be fun, so it only needs to seem smart to the player within this context.

It is fair to say that AI is a very broad topic, so implementing every possible technique isn't the plan. So, it goes without saying that we will only cover what is necessary for you to create an awesome game AI. Keep in mind, though, that we will only touch on very specific game AI techniques; the world of AI is as vast as it is great.

How AI affects the gaming experience

Players seek a realistic and immersive experience in games. AI plays a huge part in forming this gaming experience by bringing realism and fun to the virtual world. Imagine that you are accompanied by a dog as you walk around or a flock of birds scatters when you make some noise. An enemy opponent is perhaps the most common and important implementation of game AI. The few types of game AI—navigating, fighting, assisting, or analytical—add the missing elements to other players to make them feel real and challenging to compete. This dates back to when it was used most notably in Chess, Nim, Pong, and Pac-Man. Up until now, it has been used in a war frame, with procedurally built levels. As the modern game design moves quickly by introducing new features to game play, such as the open world, massive in-game characters, and social interaction, it also introduces problems because these features cause AI decision making to require more input in unpredictable environments. Even now, AAA titles have their own complications with AI that result in poor user satisfaction. We will introduce in the following sections some powerful techniques to help create this important AI module and discuss how they are implemented in Unreal Engine.

Techniques and practices of game AI

There exist many techniques to cover different aspects in game AI, from fundamental movement to advanced environment sensing and decision making. Let's look at them one by one.

Navigation

Navigation for AI is usually built up of the following tools:

- **Navigation Mesh**: Using tools such as Navigation Mesh, also known as **NavMesh**, you can designate areas in which AI can traverse. NavMesh is a simplified polygonal representation of a level (the green region in the following screenshot), where each polygon acts as a single node connected to its nearby ones. Usually, this process is automated and doesn't require designers to place nodes manually. Using special tools in Unreal, they analyze the geometry of the level and generate the most optimized Navigation Mesh accordingly. The purpose, of course, is to determine the playable areas in the level by the game agents. Note that this is the only path-finding technique available; we will use NavMesh in the examples provided in this book because it works well in this demonstration.

- **Path Following (Path nodes)**: A similar solution to NavMesh, Path nodes can designate the space in which the AI traverses:

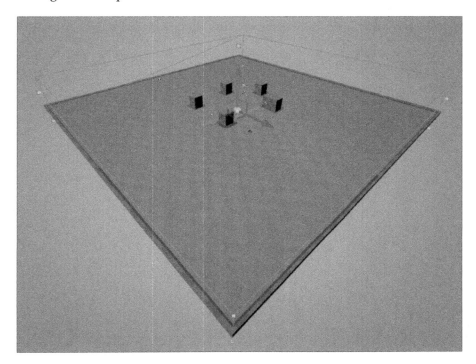

- **Behavior Tree**: Using Behavior Tree to influence your AI's next destination can create a more varied player experience. It not only calculates its requested destination, but also decides whether it should enter the screen with a cart wheeling double-back flip, no hands, or the triple somersault and jazz hands.

- **Steering behaviors**: Steering behaviors affect the way AI moves while navigating to avoid obstacles. This also means using Steering to create formations with your fleets that you have set to attack the king's wall. Steering can be used in many ways to influence the movement of the character.

- **Sensory systems**: Sensory systems can provide critical details, such as the nearby players, sound levels, nearby cover, and many other variables of the environment that can alter movement. It's critical that your AI understands the changing environment so that it doesn't break the illusion of being a real opponent.

While all these components aren't necessary to achieve AI navigation, they all provide critical feedback, which can affect the navigation. Navigating within a world is limited only by pathways within the game. We can see an example of group behavior with several members following a leader here:

Achieving realistic movement with Steering

When you think of what Steering does for a car, you would be right to imagine the same idea applied to game AI navigation. Steering influences the movement of AI as it goes to its next destination. The influences can be supplied as necessary, but we will go over the most commonly used. Avoidance is used to essentially avoid colliding with oncoming AI. Flocking is another key factor in steering and is useful in simulating interesting group movement, such as a complete panic situation, or a school of fish. The goal of Steering behaviors is to achieve realistic movement and behavior within the player's world.

Creating a character with randomness and probability

AI with character is what randomness and probability add to the bot's decision making abilities. If a bot attacked you in the same way, always entered the scene in the same way, and annoyed you with its laugh after every successful hit, it wouldn't make for a unique experience. Using randomness and probability, you can instead make the AI laugh based on probability or introduce randomness to the AI's skill of choice. Another great by-product of applying randomness and probability is that it allows you to introduce levels of difficulty or lower the chance of missing the skill cast, and even allows bots to aim more precisely. If you have bots who wander around looking for enemies, probability, and randomness could be used to work with the bot's sensory input to make a more rational decision.

Creating complex decision making with Behavior Tree

Finite State Machines (FSM) is a model to define how a finite number of states transit among each other. For example, this allows it to go from gathering to searching and then attacking, as shown in the following image. Behavior trees are similar, but they allow more flexibility. A behavior tree allows hierarchical FSM, which introduces another layer of decisions. So, the bot decides among branches of behaviors that define the state it is in. There is a tool provided by UE4 called Behavior Tree. This editor tool allows us to modify AI behavior quickly and with ease.

Here's a diagram of the FSM model:

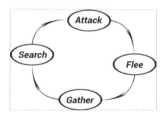

Let's take a look at the components of Behavior Tree:

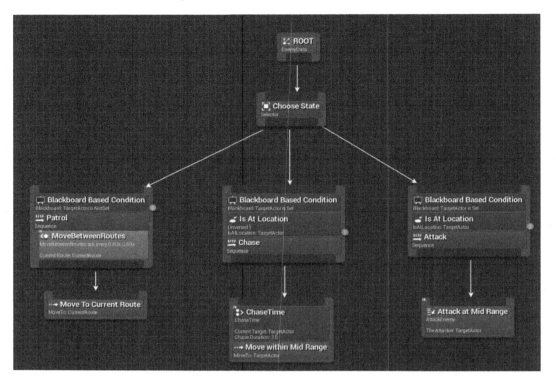

Now, we will discuss the components found within UE4 Behavior Tree.

Root

This node is the beginning node that sends the signal to the next node in the tree. This connects to a composite, which begins your first tree. What you may notice is that you are required to use a composite first to define a tree and then to create a task for this tree. This is because hierarchical FSM creates branches of states. These states will be populated with other states or tasks. This allows an easy transition among multiple states. You can see what a root node looks like as shown in the following screenshot:

Decorators

Decorators are conditional statements (the blue part on top of a node) that control whether or not a branch in the tree or even a single node can be executed. I used a decorator in the AI we will make to tell it to update to the next available route.

In the following image, you can note the **Attack & Destroy** decorator that defines the state on top of the composite. This state includes two tasks, **Attack Enemy** and **Move To Enemy**, which also has a decorator telling it to execute only when the bot state is **Search**:

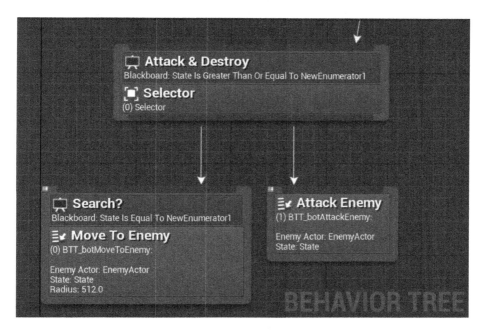

In the preceding screenshot, you can note the **Attack & Destroy** decorator that defines the state on top of the composite. This state includes two tasks, **Attack Enemy** and **Move To Enemy**, which also has a decorator telling it to execute only when the bot state is **Search**.

Composites

These are the beginning points of the states. They define how the state will behave with returns and execution flow. They have three main types: Selector, Sequence, and Simple Parallel. This beginning branch has a conditional statement, if the state is equal or greater than Search state:

Selector executes each of its children from left to right and doesn't fail; however, it returns success when one of its children returns success. So, this is good for a state that doesn't check for successfully executed nodes. The following screenshot shows an example of Selector:

Sequence executes its children in a similar fashion to Selector but returns fail when one of its children returns fail. This means that it's required that all nodes return success to complete the sequence. You can see a Sequence node in the following screenshot:

Last but not least, Simple Parallel allows you to execute a task and a tree essentially at the same time. This is great for creating a state that requires another task to always be called. To set it up, you need to first connect it to a task that it will execute. The second task or state connected continues to be called with the first task until the first task returns success.

Services

Services run as long as the composite it is added to stays activated. They tick at the intervals you set within the properties. They have another float property called Tick Interval that allows you to control how often this service is executed in the background. Services are used to modify the state of AI in most cases because it's always called. For example, in the bot that we will create, we will add a service to the first branch of the tree so that it's called without interruption and will be able to maintain the state that the bot should be in at any given movement. The green node in the following screenshot is a service with important information explicitly:

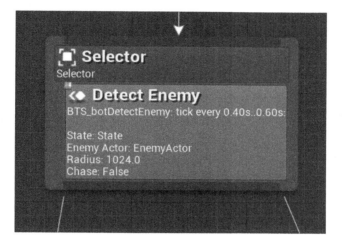

This service, called **Detect Enemy**, actually runs a deviating cycle that updates Blackboard variables such as **State** and **Enemy Actor**.

Tasks

Tasks do the dirty work and report success or failed if it's necessary. They have blueprint nodes that can be referred to in Behavior Tree. There are two types of nodes that you'll use most often when working with Task: Event Receive Execute, which receives the signal to execute the connected scripts, and Finish Execute, which sends the signal back and returns `true` or `false` on success. This is important when making a task meant for the Sequence composite node.

Blackboard

A Blackboard is an asset to store the variables to be used within the AI Behavior Tree. They are created outside Behavior Tree. In our example, we will store an enumeration variable for the state in the **State**, **EnemyActor** object to hold the currently targeted enemy, and **Route** to store the current route position that the AI is requested to travel to, just to name a few. You can see all current variables as keys in **Blackboard** panel as follows:

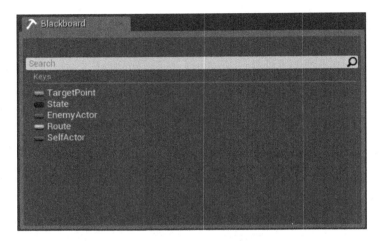

They work just by setting a public variable of a node to one of the available Blackboard variables in the drop-down menu. The naming convention in the following screenshot makes this process streamlined:

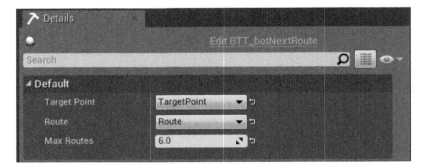

Sensory systems

A sensory system usually consists of several modules, such as sight, sound, and memory, to help the AI capture information about the environment. A bot can maintain the illusion of intelligence using sounds within their environment to make a deliberate risk assessment before engaging a hazardous threat or aiding a nearby teammate who is calling for help. The use of memory will allow the bot to avoid an area where it remembers seeing a severe threat or rush back to an area where it last saw its group. Creating a sensory system in the case of an enemy player is heavily based on the environment where the AI fights the player. It needs to be able to find cover, evade the enemy, get ammo, and other features that you feel create immersive AI for your game. A game with AI that challenges the player creates a unique individual experience. A good sensory system contributes critical information that makes for reactive AI. In this project, we will use the sensory system to detect the pawns that the AI can see. We will also use functions to check for the line of sight of the enemy. We will check whether there is another pawn in the way of our path. We can check for cover and other resources within the area.

Machine learning

Machine learning is a branch on its own. This technique allows AI to learn from situations and simulations. Inputs are taken from the environment, including the context in which the bot allows it to make decisive actions. In machine learning, the inputs are put within a classifier that can predict a set of outputs with a certain level of certainty. Classifiers can be combined into ensembles to increase the accuracy of probabilistic prediction. We won't dig deep into this subject, but there exist a vast amount of resources for studying machine learning, ranging from text books (*Pattern Recognition and Machine Learning* by *Christopher M. Bishop, Springer*) to online courses (*Machine Learning* on coursera.org).

Tracing

Tracing allows another actor within the world to detect objects by ray tracing. A single line trace is sent out, and if it collides with an actor, the actor is returned along with information on the impact. Tracing is used for many reasons; one way it is used in FPS is to detect hits. Are you familiar with the hit box? When your player shoots in a game, a trace is shot out that collides with the opponent's hit box, determining the damage to the player, and if you're skillful enough, it results in death. Other shapes available for traces, such as spheres, capsules, and boxes, allow tracing for different situations. Recently, I used Box Trace for my car to detect objects near it.

Influence Mapping

Influence Mapping isn't a finite approach; it's the idea that specific locations on the map would be attributed information that directly influences the player or AI. An example of using Influence Mapping with AI is presence falloff. Let's say we have other enemy AI in a group; their presence map would create a radial circle around the group with the intensity based on the size of the group. This way, the other AI knows by entering this area that they're entering a zone occupied by other enemy AI.

Practical information isn't the only thing people use it for, so just understand that it's meant to provide another level of input to help your bot make more additional decisions. As shown in the following image, different colors represent zones occupied by different types of AI, and color intensity indicates the influence with respect to each AI character:

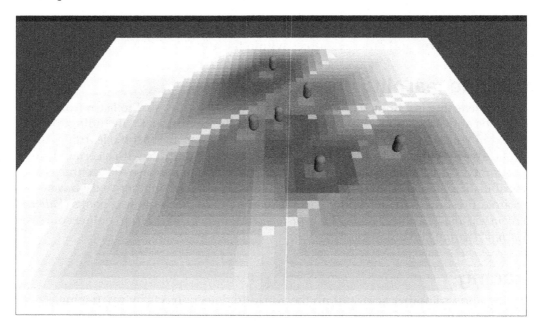

Practical information isn't the only thing people use it for, so just understand that it's meant to provide another level of input to help your bot make more additional decisions.

Unreal Engine 4 tools

Unreal Engine 4 provides a complete suite of tools to add common AI capability to your game. We will go into the details of each tool within this book. Here is a list of the tools that are covered:

- **Behavior Tree**: This is used to create different states and the logic behind AI.
- **Navigation Component**: This handles movement for AI.
- **Blackboard Asset**: These are used to store information. They act as the local variable for AI.
- **Enumeration**: This is used to create states, which you can alternate between.
- **Target Point**: Our Waypoints class is derived from the Target Point class, which we will use to create a basic form of Path node.
- **AI Controller and Character**: This controller will handle communication between the world and controlled pawn for AI.
- **Navigation Volumes**: This is used to create Navigation Mesh in the environment to enable Path Finding for AI.

Let's look at the following screenshot:

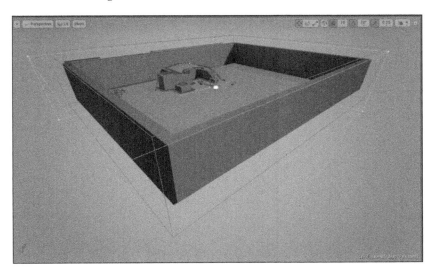

There are two types of NavMesh volume. The first, the NavMesh Bounds volume, defines the area for NavMesh. The Nav Modifier volume, when supplied with a Nav Area class, affects the NavMesh Bounds volume's navigation attributes where the two intersect.

Summary

In this chapter, we started by introducing game AI and discussing why it is important for our gaming experience. Then, we illustrated most of the used game AI techniques and what they are capable of. The corresponding UE4 tools for game AI were also mentioned to provide a bigger picture of the content we will cover throughout this book. In the next chapter, we will create our basic AI by setting up an AI-controlled player and adding some simple behavior to it.

2
Creating Basic AI

In this chapter, we will create our first AI step-by-step and talk about the techniques that we demonstrate along the way. So today, we will dive right into Unreal Engine 4 using the bare components needed to create a single state with random movement for your AI. We will then review what we've done, the changes we can make, and the disadvantages of the techniques demonstrated.

This chapter will cover:

- Setting up our project
- Creating the AIController
- Sending instructions to Pawn with the AIController
- Creating small blueprint scripts to assist in navigation

Goal

Our goal for this chapter is to place an AI character in the level that has the blueprint to instruct it to move randomly and indefinitely. We will demonstrate multiple techniques throughout this chapter to get a good grasp of some really basic AI techniques commonly featured in titles. These techniques are listed as follows:

- First, we want to place an AI character, Hero, in the level that has the blueprint to instruct it to move randomly and indefinitely. We will achieve this by first creating a new third-person project and naming it appropriately. We will then use the default pawn provided from the sample content as the bot. We will create an AIController to control our pawn. We will then provide our AIController with instructions to move our bot randomly and indefinitely.

- Second, we want to make the AI character follow some basic path. For example, we'll have the AI move along the walls in one direction. We can take our existing project and modify the AIController with new instructions. From there, our AI will now move along the walls in one direction indefinitely.

- Third, we want to make a new enemy AI character that will chase the first AI character we made—that is, Hero.

 We will have to make additional changes to Hero to give it the ability to run directly away from Enemy.

Enemy will simply be instructed to move toward Hero every second.

Setting up the project

Let's open up Unreal Engine 4! We will begin with the first process of creating a new project.

 We will use Unreal Engine 4.6.0 throughout this book. The instructions may vary per version. We will present the idea behind our actions as we demonstrate them using Unreal Engine 4; so, hopefully, you will be able to translate the instructions as you see fit.

Here, we will use the Third Person Shooter template, which allows us to easily observe how the character moves in the environment. Perform the following steps:

1. Go to the **New Project** window if you aren't there already:

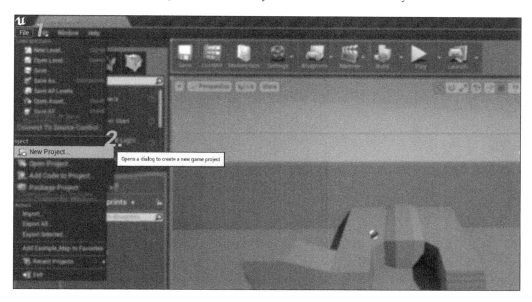

2. Select the **Third Person** blueprint project:

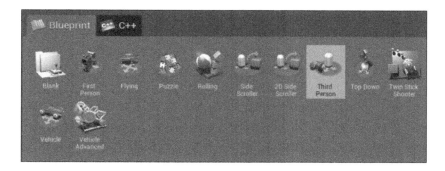

3. Name your project as you see fit; I've named mine `ImprovedAI`. Then, hit **Create Project** in the lower-right corner of the window.

Environment

Even though we are using the Third Person blueprint template, these techniques can be used on other templates as well. You must adapt what you learn here. That being said, what you start to understand is that these techniques are tools. Understanding how to create a state, sensory component, navigation component, and so on is generally perceived to be the same thing, but what is used, and how it is used, is dictated by the AI environment.

Prerequisites

Note that my windows and function names are different. I will run you through my settings so that you can have the same setup as I do. Here are the steps to perform:

1. Let's go to **General | Appearance** within **Editor Preferences** and under **User Interface**, select the **User Small Tool Bar Icons** option and unselect the **Show Friendly Variable Names** option. Your settings should look like the following screenshot:

2. Navigate to the **Blueprints** folder within the project:

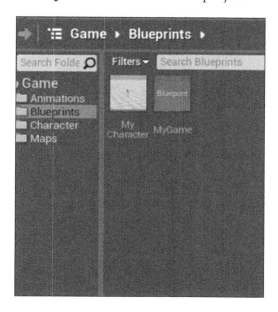

3. Now we will possess our pawn. Right-click and hit the **Blueprint** option to create a blueprint:

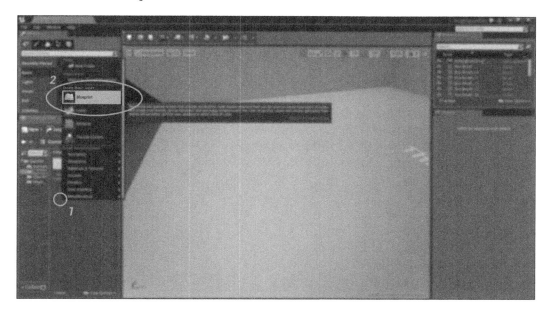

4. Next, we will create our **AIController** class. Go to **Custom Classes** and type `AIController`. Select it and then click on **Select**, as shown in the following screenshot:

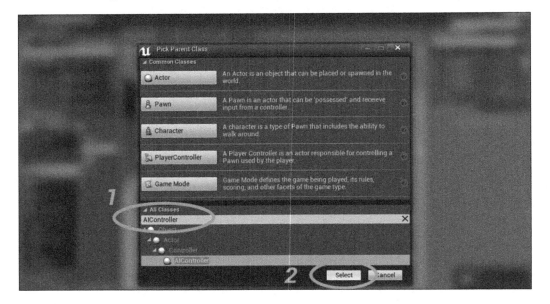

This will create the blueprint, and I named it `MyController` here.

Using our new AIController class

Ever notice how one player can be any character they desire? This is the hierarchy that creates the pawn and the controller. The controller is what the player inherits after waiting for some time in the game lobby. It is used to manage the input and connection from the player. This class comes with additional functions to help navigate the bot and the ability to assign a Behavior Tree to the controller. In this demonstration, we will cover some of the basics of the AIController class.

Assigning the AIController class

So, now that we have what we need to create an AI, we will assign the
`MyController` class to the `MyCharacter` base. To do so, go to the **Defaults** section
within the `MyCharacter` blueprint. Search for **AIController Class** and set it to
`MyController`, as shown in the following screenshot:

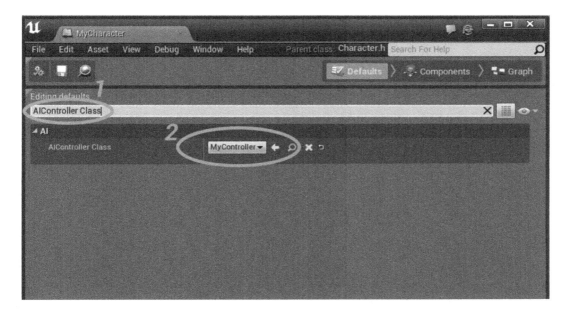

When a character isn't possessed, it will automatically be possessed by AIController.
So, with the change we just made, the default AIController class that possesses our
`MyCharacter` blueprint will be `MyController`.

Placing the pawn

It's assumed you understand such a simple task! Let's place our newly set up pawn into the bright beautiful world by dragging and dropping it from **Content Browser**:

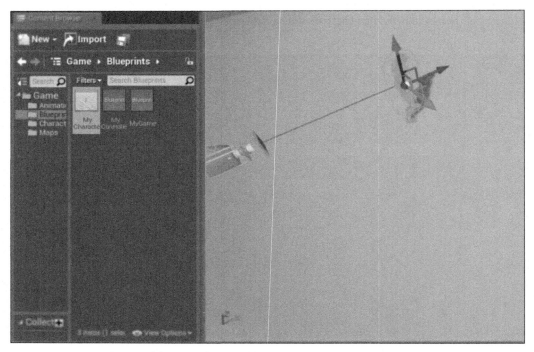

Drag and drop MyCharacter blueprint to the level to create a pawn

There is a long line of people who have lost work to crashes and other mishaps; if you would like to join them, please skip this step. Otherwise, navigate to **File | Save All** whenever you make some significant new changes to the level.

Sending the instructions

Now that we have our project set up and saved—or not saved for our brave fellows—let's move forward to the fun part: blueprints! Let's take a look at the steps to send the instructions:

1. Open your `MyController` blueprint within **Content Browser** and zoom in to the **EventGraph**:

   So, the plan is to have our bot move around randomly. This will be built in a simple fashion, so we will do the computing by hand.

2. First, let's create an **Event Tick** node that will be triggered in every frame as the game runs.

3. We will add a **Delay** node to receive signals from **Event Tick** to set the **Duration** pin to **1**.

4. Next, we will add a **Move To Location** node, which will signal the `AIController` class to tell its pawn to move to the destination point specified.

5. As we didn't use **Path Finding** at this time, which is a subject we will touch upon later, go to the **MoveToLocation** node and set **bUsePathFinding** to false or leave it unselected.

   The **EventGraph** for your `MyController` class should look similar to the following screenshot:

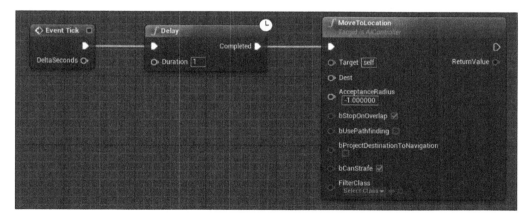

6. With the **MoveToLocation** node ready, we now need to supply it with a random location. We will grab the current location of the controlled pawn, create an additional vector with a random value of -255 to 255 for the **X** and **Y** variables, leaving **Z** to **0.0**. Then, we will add the location from the controlled pawn to the vector we just created. You should have a blueprint similar to the following setup:

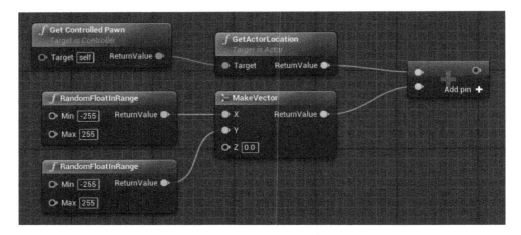

7. Let's finalize this and move this new random location blueprint to the **MoveToLocation** node that we set up previously. Now, let's connect the results of the addition of the two vectors to the destination of the **MoveToLocation** node. With this done, you should have a blueprint setup similar to the following preview:

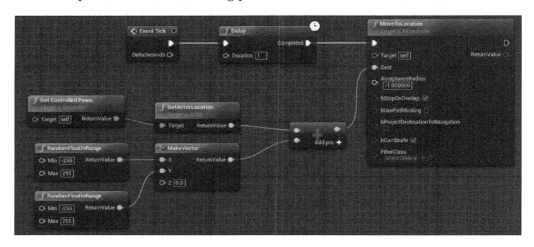

Save it all!

Small tips on MoveToLocation

Here are some basic tips on **MoveToLocation**:

- **AcceptanceRadius**: This allows you to increase the radius that is acceptable for a completed move. Let's suppose that there is an enemy holding a sword who wants to attack the player. The **AcceptanceRadius** option will help you define how far this enemy should be standing away from his target—ideally 1 meter—and then perform an attack animation to swing the sword.

- **bStopOnOverlap**: This tells your bot to stop if it overlaps the point rather than going precisely there. This will take into consideration the radius of the collision mesh attached to the bot.

- **bUsePathFinding**: If this is selected, the bot will use the **NavMesh** option to find its destination. If unselected, the bot will simply move in a straight line to the destination, not taking into account any obstacles. This helps save the performance in some situations.

- **bProjectDestinationToNavigation**: This projects the location on the navigation data before using it. This helps validate the target actor's location—that is, whether it exists on a playable area or not.

- **bCanStrafe**: This determines whether the AI can transverse diagonally on **NavMesh** or not.

- **FilterClass**: This allows you to use **AreaClass**, which is another navigation component that affects the navigation of the AI. This effects changes such as exclusion or exclusive access to areas of **NavMesh** and alters the navigation cost.

Reviewing the current progress

You can wipe the sweat from your forehead; the hard work has yet to begin. So, what have we done so far?

- We've set up our AI project
- We've set up our pawn with our new AIController
- We've sent instructions to our pawn using AIController

We're halfway there. This simple setup allows us to put all our instructions on our AIController, which will possess the pawn we created from the sample content. The AIController is assigned to pawns, which means that multiple pawns can share the same AIController.

As we can see, our AI now runs indefinitely. Perfect! Let's move on to the second section of this chapter!

Adding the challenge

Now, we will add line traces to the AI character. In our demonstration, we will use traces to detect the wall in front of the pawn. Other examples of using traces in the AI include Line of Sight checking, getting surface rotation, and getting nearby actors.

Let's go back to Unreal Engine Level Editor and look within **Content Browser**. Perform the following steps:

1. Rename our `MyController` blueprint `Hero`; this will act as the player in this scenario.

2. Open our `Hero` blueprint and go to the **EventGraph** section.

3. Now, remove every node except the **Event Tick** and **Move to Location** nodes. We will replace these with new blueprint scripting:

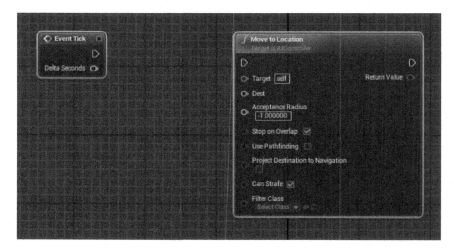

Blueprint after removing unnecessary nodes

4. Pull from the return exec pin on the **Event Tick** node and create a **Delay** node.

5. Set the **Duration** value to **.05** so that it will update relatively fast.

6. Now, we have to get the location from the pawn to create line traces. We will also use the right vector to face the pawn to the right from the pawn's current rotation when the collision ahead is detected.

7. Right-click on **EventGraph** and search for **Get Controlled Pawn**.

8. From the **Return Value** pin of **Get Controlled Pawn**, pull the **Get Actor Location** node.

9. From the **Return Value** pin of **GetActorLocation**, pull a vector and then drop it in an empty area.

10. Search for **LineTraceByChannel**, which is located under the **Collision** category, as shown in the following screenshot:

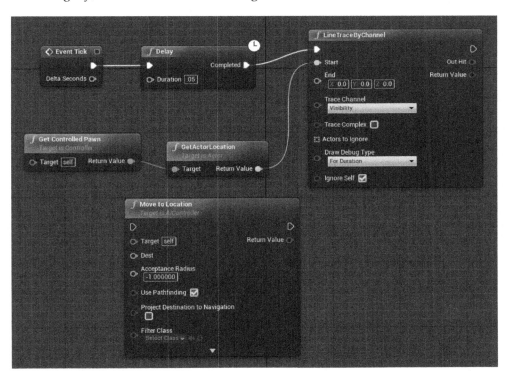

Traces

We will use this to trace from the player's location to 255 units in front of the character. If anything collides with the trace, we will face the pawn to the right based on the pawn's rotation. This simple check will be enough to make our bot run along the walls indefinitely; so, perform the following steps:

1. Pull the **Return Value** pin from **GetActorLocation** and drop it. Then, search for Vector + Vector.

2. We now need to select **Get Controlled Pawn** and pull **Get Actor Forward Vector** from it. This contains vector information going in the direction that is in front of our pawn.

3. So we will multiply **Return Value** by **255**. This is the vector we want to add to the actor's location. This results in adding 255 units in the direction ahead of the pawn's current location.

4. Now, we need to take the results of the addition of the **End** pin for the **LineTraceByChannel** node. This will trace directly in front of our pawn:

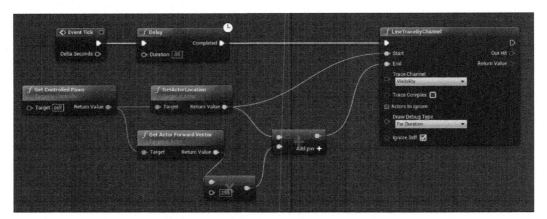

5. Pull from the Vector + Vector node again, and this time we will plug it into the **Dest** pin for the **Move to Location** node. This will move the character forward indefinitely:

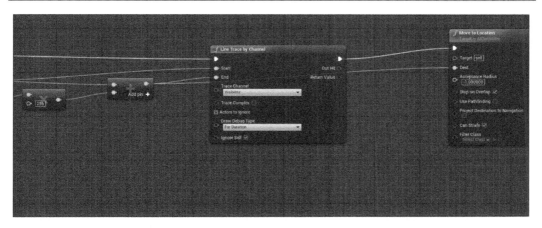

Let's try this out! Hit **Simulate** and look at your character move forward indefinitely! The only problem is that it can't avoid the walls just yet. We will change this by introducing a **Select Vector** node that chooses a different direction when a collision is detected by **Line Trace**:

6. Once more, we will pull from the **Get Controlled Pawn** node and search for **Get Actor Right Vector**.

7. From this node, we will pull the vector and multiply it by **512**.

8. We will add this to the pawn's current location. So, similar to what we did before going forward, we will add 512 units to the right of the pawn's current location:

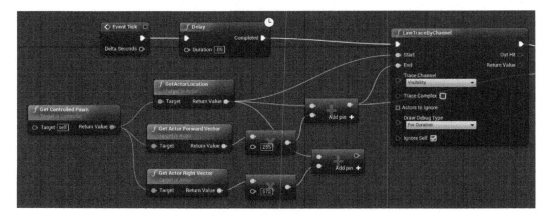

9. Right-click on the **EventGraph** section and search for **Select Vector**.

10. From the **LineTraceByChannel** node, pull **Return Value** and connect it to the **Select Vector** node. Then, select **A**.

11. Now, pull from the right location to **A** of the **Select Vector** node.

12. Then, pull from the forward location to **B** of the **Select Vector** node.

13. Select the **Select Vector** node and pull from **Return Value** into the **Dest** pin of **Move to Location**.

14. Select the nodes and create a comment:

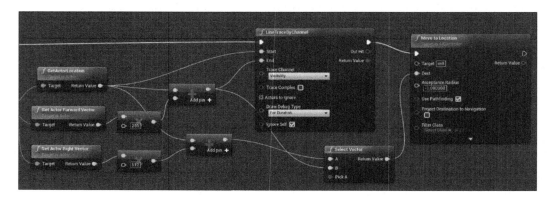

Let's see how this looks in-game:

It seems to work perfectly! This will create the chase for the next addition to this project.

Reviewing the current progress

So now, we've created our Hero character, who isn't much of a hero as he runs indefinitely, but that is another story. Here is the current round of the changes:

- We've updated the AI instructions
- We've demonstrated a basic sensory component

Now, let's move on to creating the Enemy AI.

The Enemy logic

Enemy needs to be able to find and run toward Hero. We will achieve this by searching for the Hero character, calculating the difference in direction, and facing Enemy toward Hero.

Adding the Enemy AI

Let's go back to Unreal Engine and focus on **Content Browser**. We now need an opponent. To add this, follow these steps:

1. Right-click and select **Blueprint**.
2. At the lower end of the window, let's drop all the classes and search for **AIController**.
3. Select **AIController** under **Controller** and hit **Select** in the lower-right corner.
4. We will name this **AIController** Enemy.
5. Open Enemy **AIController** and go to the **EventGraph** section.

First, we must find Hero and then store it in a local variable to be used at any time. To do so, follow these steps:

1. Right-click in an empty area within **EventGraph** and search for **Event Begin Play**.
2. Pull from the exec pin and search for **Get All Actors Of Class**.
3. Set the **Actor Class** pin to **Hero**.

4. Pull from the **Out Actors** array and search for **ForEachLoopWithBreak**:

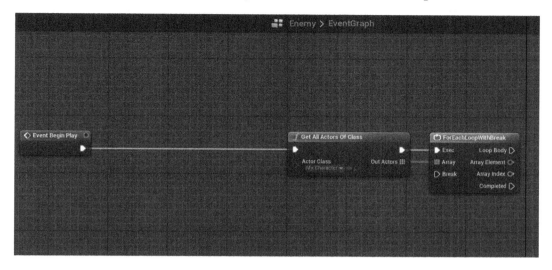

We want a filter for the Hero class within the MyCharacter pawn returned. To do so, follow these steps:

1. Pull from the **Array Element** pin and search for **Cast to MyCharacter**.
2. Then, pull from the **As My Character** pin and search for **Get Controller**.
3. Get the class of the controller using the **Get Class** node.
4. Compare the Hero class with the **Class = Class** node.
5. Pull from the return of **Equal** and create a **Branch** node.
6. From the **Loop Body** pin, link the newly created branch.
7. From the **True** exec pin of the **Branch** node, create the **SET** node.
8. Then, pull from the pure cast to the **SET** node we just created.

9. We want to comment this and call this section `Find Hero`:

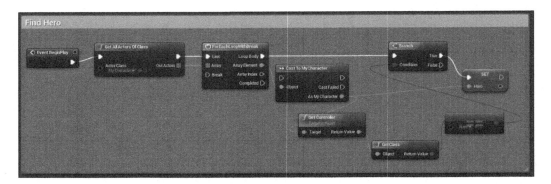

We now have to constantly update the Enemy instructions to moving toward the fleeing Hero character. Note that there are that nodes that can directly achieve this, such as **Simple Move to Actor, AI MoveTo**, and so on. We will implement similar behavior to give you a look at how this can be done under the hood. Perform the following steps:

1. Right-click on the **EventGraph** section and search for **Event Tick**.

2. From the exec pin, drop and search for **Delay**.

3. Set the **Duration** pin to **.05** seconds.

4. Pull from **Completed** and create a new node **Move to Location**:

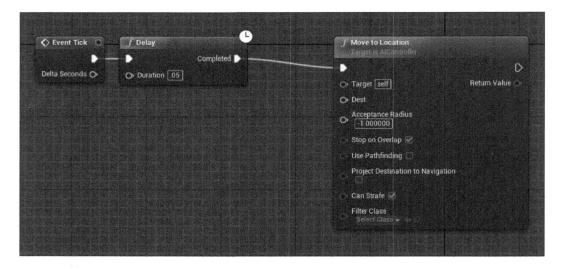

Now, we need to get the direction from Enemy to Hero and move Enemy in this direction. We can do this thus:

1. Get the `Hero` variable and drop it near the **Delay** node.

2. From the `Hero` variable, get the actor's location.

3. Pull from **Return Value** of the **GetActorLocation** node, drop it, and search for **Get Direction Vector**.

4. Now, right-click and search for **Get Controlled Pawn**.

5. Pull from the **Return Value** pin of **Get Controlled Pawn** and **GetActorLocation**.

6. Then, pull from the **Return Value** pin of the **GetActorLocation** node and plug it into the **From** pin in the **Get Direction Vector** node.

7. Pull from the **Return Value** pin of the **Get Direction Vector** node and **Make Rot from X**.

8. Pull from **Make Rot From X** and **Get Forward Vector**.

9. Now, from **Get Forward Vector**, we will multiply it by **255** to get 255 units in the forward vector direction.

10. Lastly, we will add this to the **GetActorLocation** node of the Hero pawn.

11. The result of the addition is the destination for **Move to Location**:

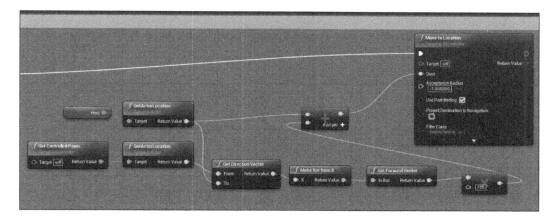

12. Now, place a comment around this and name it `Chase Hero`.

Save it all!

Now, head back to the **Viewport** section and hit **Simulate**. You should now see our Hero character is running forward and turning right when it detects an obstacle in its way. Our Enemy character is chasing fast behind our Hero character. Now, imagine if you were in the Hero character's place; you would be in complete fear!

Summary

What we demonstrated here is how you can create an Enemy AI that pursues a player or another AI. This type of behavior can be used to create a challenge and provide the player with feedback, which results in a better gameplay experience. AI can definitely be more complicated, but this should only be done if it is needed to improve the play experience. In the next chapter, we will add randomness and probability to our AI character to make it behave in a more interesting way.

3
Adding Randomness and Probability

In this chapter, we will introduce randomness and probability techniques that can be used to add randomness, chance, and character to AI, which would otherwise be perfect. We will start with a quick "Probability 101" to explain some basic concepts; then, we will demonstrate how to use Stream to control a non-uniform distribution of numbers and use these results to demonstrate probability. We will cover how these are used within Unreal Engine 4. Finally, we will build on top of our enemy AIController to have it randomly perform an action.

This chapter will cover:

- Probability, probability distribution, and non-uniform distribution
- Using RandomStream in UE4 to add randomness to our AI
- Adding random behavior to enemy AI-based states

Introducing probability

We know an event will occur, but how often will it occur? This is how we can quantify probability, and this is what we will use to control the frequency of an outcome. So, let's say we flip a quarter. The event we know will occur is heads (H), but it can still land on tails (T). So, the way we would write the probability of landing on heads is $P\ (H) = ?$

At this point, we know that heads will occur, although we still don't know how often it will occur. To understand this, we must first get the number of possible outcomes that meet our conditions, which is 1 for heads. Then, we must get the number of events that are equally likely to occur, which is 2. So, now we need to put this in the equation for probability:

# of possible met conditions / # of equality likely outcomes

If we do some basic math and break it down further, we will have 50%:

P (H) = 1/2 = 50%

So what this says is, if you flipped a coin a million or even a billion times, the more the number of times you flip it, the closer it will get to 50% of the events landing equally on heads and on tails. This is useful when controlling the chance that a function will execute.

In our example, we will demonstrate a lottery-type probability. We determined that we have a 20% chance of getting gold, which translates to a decimal of .2. We will generate a random number from 0 through 1. We get .19, and we're in the money! We roll again, and we get .57, we're out of money!

These are some ways to control the execution flow of your AI. You could also apply this to other behaviors that are directly linked to the traits of the specific AI. So, if this character is of a certain class, certain monsters may be more frightened by this class of characters.

Probabilistic distribution

A probabilistic distribution of numbers means that we will know the finite numbers of equal outcomes. So, we would use this if, for example, we had a monster with a lot of weapons. We don't want all of the weapons to drop if the monster dies. Although, if we just applied a simple rule to limit the number of weapons dropped, there is still an equal chance that they could get the rare sword versus the crappy sword that no one wants.

Say we applied probabilistic distribution to the selection of weapons. Here is the scenario. We have 50% items ranked crappy through okay and 35% items ranked well through best, ending with rare items at 15%. Now, we will generate a random number of weapons they can get, and the individual items selected will be generated with probabilistic distribution.

Non-uniform distribution

A non-uniform distribution of numbers means that we will not know the finite number of outcomes. We know that 0 through 1 will be generated but not whether 0 or 1 is more likely to be generated. With this said, this is perfect for creating many unpredictable scenarios. In UE4, we have the typical Random and RandomStream tool. The explicit difference between the two is the fact that we can control the seed that generates our random output.

So, to say it another way, non-uniform distribution is a random generation of numbers that are not equally likely to occur. The true behavior of randomness can be replicated but at the cost of time and efficiency. So, we've come up with algorithms to generate random numbers. One of the tools that UE4 provides to generate random numbers is RandomStream.

RandomStream in Unreal Engine 4

Say you want to freeze the randomly generated trees you've made. Typically, when using a random node from UE4's artillery, this information will be lost once you exit the game. With RandomStream, you can actually save the seed that generated the random output and load the same random output by calling on this seed. So in UE4, you will find a blueprint node called Make RandomStream. This node has one input pin called Initial Seed.

The reason we use a seed is because this is a pseudo random-number generator. This means that the numbers are calculated and are deterministic. Pseudo means that we will use algorithms to calculate the randomness; however, by calculating the randomness, we technically know what it will be beforehand, thus making it deterministic. The contrast is true randomness, which captures noise from a forest, waterfalls, the atmosphere, or even a TV channel. The reason this will be indefinitely more random is that the noise captured is unlikely to ever repeat, as with many things in life. With calculations, there is always a capacity because the task is to replicate the phenomenon at a fraction of the cost. Initially, when we created computers, memory was very important—it still is. But at this point, we created algorithms to replace the need for storing noise, but we would rather have a key or seed as we are more familiar with them. The reason for which it can be considered a key is that, by having it, two people on separate computers can generate identical random numbers.

Now technically, if we were to increase the length of the seed to something exponentially high, it would be practically infinitely random. You have to add this because we know that there is a definite end, while with life there is no finite end. So in UE4, randomizing the seed will directly affect the randomness of the numbers calculated. This is what I do to create practically unpredictable randomness.

The plan

We will continue from where we left off in *Chapter 2, Creating Basic AI*, and continue to make changes to our two AIControllers. In the past chapter, we set up our Enemy to chase our Hero indefinitely. In this chapter, we will introduce another state to our Enemy AI, which will allow it to either run away from us or run toward us. This represents the Enemy attacking us or fleeing, depending on the shock probability when we encounter the Enemy.

Let's get started!

Adding Wander

Here, we will define three states of AI. This will make it easier when specifying actions in different states. Now, the first state we will add is Wander. It will make the AI move randomly and indefinitely. This will be the initial state of the AI, and it will be capable of transitioning into other states once we approach the AI. The other two states are the two reactions that we give the AI. The idea is that when we approach the AI, there is a chance that it will flee or attack. The chance is the probability that we determined and created in the blueprint.

Setting up the project

Let's open Unreal Engine 4! Perform the following steps:

1. First, we have to change our Enemy to act as a wandering frightened monster. So, double-click on the **Enemy** AIController. Now, navigate to **Event Graph** and zoom in.

2. We want to create a new variable for **State** and make this **Integer**.

3. Next, we have to change the **Find Hero** script. We will adapt this to detect the Hero. What we also want to keep is the chasing of the Hero blueprint. This will be used to chase or run from us scared, which is the inverse. So, focus on the script.

4. Remove **Event Begin Play** from the beginning of the script. Next, pull back **Event Tick** from the **Chase Hero** script.

5. Replace the **Delay** node that is after the **Event Tick** node in the **Chase Hero** script and put a **Switch on Int** node. Then, pull the **State** variable and connect it to the **Selection** value pin:

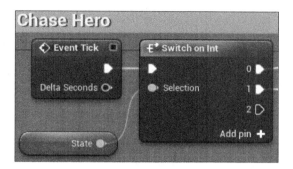

 Switch on Int is a very useful function. I've used it countless times to replace the redundant work that you could usually do in passes, such as recurring a task a number a times before going to the next index.

6. Now, the AI will constantly tick based on **State**. Different scripts are executed, which can be transitioned in between, and this is the basis for Finite State Machine.

7. Next, let's conjoin our two scripts to the **Switch on Int** node. We want the **Find Hero** script to be connected to the index **0** of the node. Then, connect index **1** of the node to the **Chase Hero** script. So, you can press *Ctrl* and click on index **0**, moving **Move to Location** to index **1** after connecting index **0** to **Get All Actors Of Class**.

8. So, we have to check the distance of the Actors element found from **Get All Actors Of Class**, and then, if an Actor is within range, we will roll the chance of transiting into Attacking or Running away from this Actor:

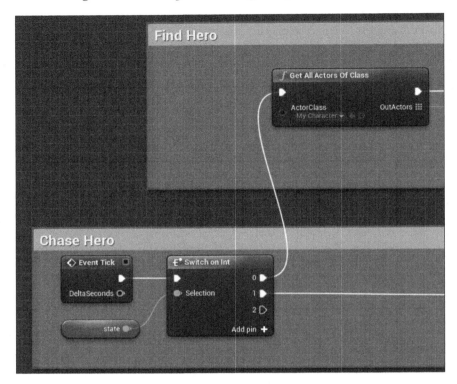

9. Now, focus on **ForEachLoopWithBreak**, and let's check the current Actor element for distance using the **Get Horizontal Distance To** node. Place this node and **Get Controlled Pawn** and connect this to the **Target** pin of **Get Horizontal Distance To**.

10. From the **Array Element** pin, connect to **Other Actor** of **Get Horizontal Distance To**. The distance we want the Actor within is 512 units. So, pull from **Return Value**, type the less than (<) symbol, and compare it to 512. Once more, what we want to do is ensure that we don't ever run from ourselves.

11. Compare **Array Element** node to **Get Controlled Pawn** using a **Not Equal** node. Then, create an **AND** gate node and join both the Boolean results. Create a **Branch** node from the results from the **AND** gate node. This **Branch** node should be after **Get Horizontal Distance To**.

Creating probability

The Blueprint script we are about to create demonstrates a simple yet effective probability. The system works off the idea of the simple lottery probability of 0-1 with a variant. So, you first determined the chance that **TRUE** will return from the function. Next, you determined the range that the lottery will span for, which is 1 by default. The rest is left to the script. It now takes **Change Weight**, and **Number Span** then calculates an offset. From there, we will calculate a range of probabilities from **Chance Weight**. Then, we will generate a random number within the range of our **Number Span** and check whether it's within the range of the probability we determined before. This small variant makes the probability less predictable. The following image shows the simple lottery probability script checking for a random value within the determined probability range:

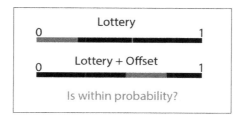

Note **Offset** from **Lottery** in the second one, which lands as true. Next time, the range of probability will not be there, and a new random value will be calculated.

Non-uniform distribution with RandomStream

The first thing we want to do is initialize RandomStream. We can do this by creating a **Make RandomStream** node and populating the initial seed pin with a random integer in Range. RandomStream allows us to control the random generation of output. If we do not change the seed within RandomStream, it will constantly produce the same results. So, with that in mind, we must constantly reset the seed within the stream so that the random output changes. Perform the following steps:

1. Focusing back to the Enemy AIController, create **Random Integer** in **Range** and set the **Max** value to 65535. Then, pull from **Return Value** and type Make RandomStream.

2. Now, we need to create variables to update RandomStream. Create an **Offset** float with a default value of **0**. Then, create a **ChanceWeight** float with a default value of **.25**. Create a **Max N** float with a default value of **1**.

3. Then, create **Event Begin Play**. Drag out the **Offset** variable and make a **SET** node. Drag from the exec pin of **Event Begin Play** to the **SET** node you just created. Next, create **Random Float in Range from Stream** and pull from **Return Value** to the **Offset** Float:

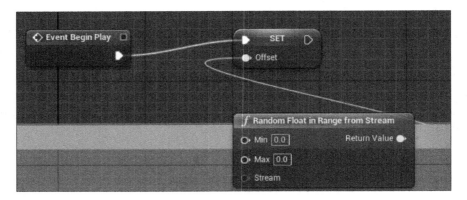

4. We now need to plug in our RandomStream to this node and connect the **Max N** variable to the **Max** Float of **Random Float in Range from Stream**. This will now create a random offset at the beginning of the game.

5. Now, let's start the probability script. Let's get our variable and create **Random Float in Range from Stream**. Then, we want to create two nodes from this to compare **Return Value**. We want to check whether the value is greater than or less than. Then, pull a pin and create an **AND** logic gate. Finally, pull the other Boolean compare.

6. Next, pull the result of **AND** to a new **Branch** node. What we need to do next is compare the random result to **Lottery Probability Range** we calculated using **Offset**:

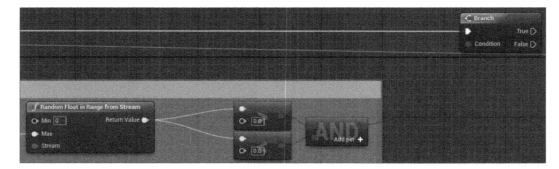

7. So, get **Offset** from the variables. We want to put this in modulo (%) and then connect it out to the greater than (>) compare node.

8. Next, we want to get **ChanceWeight** from the variables. Then, we will multiply this by the **Max N** value to calculate the probability range. We will do two things with the results of this calculation, as in the next steps.

9. First, we want to get the difference from the **Max N** value with the results. Then, we will connect this to modulo (%).

10. Next, we want to add the probability range to the results of modulo (%). Then, we will pipe this into a clamp for safety. We will set the **Min** value to **0** and **Max** to **Max N**. The results of this clamp plugs into the less than (<) of the compare node shown as follows:

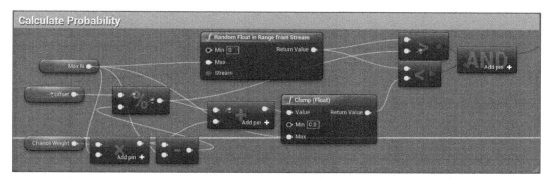

Creating transitions

Transitions help apply the appropriate actions to what's being perceived in the AI's environment. They also continue the execution flow, and this is what makes Finite State Machines so special. We will apply this in our project by transiting into Flee or Attack state, and after sometime, it will calculate whether it should flee or continue attacking. Once no enemy is found, the AI will transition back into a wandering state. Follow these steps:

1. So, from the **Branch** node we last created, let's set our **State** variable on our **True** pin for the **Branch** node. Then, we will set another **State** variable on the **False** pin for the **Branch** node. From there, let's set the **True Set State** value to **1**, then **False Set State** to **2**.

2. Next, let's rename our **Hero** variable to **Target** just to make it easier. Next, we want to set **Target** after our two other **Set State** variables.

3. Then, we want to connect both the **Set State** variable nodes to the **Set Target** variable node. The **Set Target** node should be set to **Break the ForEachLoopWithBreak**.

4. Now to reset the RandomStream. Let's zoom out and find the **Event Tick** node. From there, let's pull pin and create **Sequence** between **Switch on Int**.

5. From **then_1** of the **Sequence** node, let's create **Delay** with **Duration** of **0.2** second. Then, pull from **Return Value** of **Make Random Stream** and find **Reset Random Stream**. This will reset the stream, and if you have **Random Integer** in **Range** connected as we do, it will generate a new random **Int** each time it's reset.

6. Plug this in after **Delay** so that the reset happens every second. Then, we want to pull from reset to the **offset** variable of the **SET** node we created from **Event**:

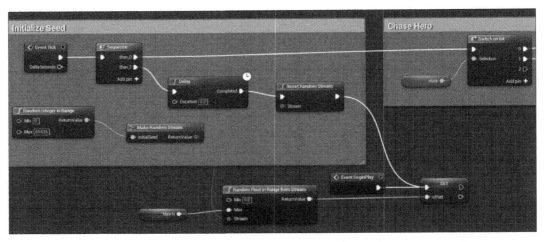

Set offset to a random value

7. Now, let's create a new **Sequence** node by pulling from index **1** of the **Switch on Int** node. Then, connect index **2** of the **Switch on Int** node to the **Sequence** node from before.

8. Now, let's pull from **Then 1** of the **Sequence** node and create a **Delay** node. This node will transition our AI back to the Wandering state from where it can detect Enemy again.

9. So, let's create **Random Float in Range from Stream** and connect **Stream** to **Random Stream**, which we created earlier. Then, set the **Min** value to **3** and the **Max** value to **5**.

10. After the **Delay** node, set the **State** variable to **0**. Then, set **Target** to none:

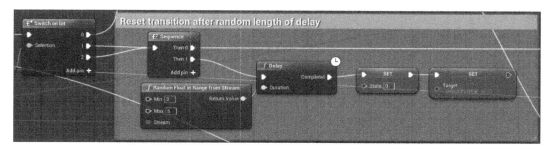

Fleeing and attacking

So, we will take from our old bit and add a small change, which will make the character run away from the Target instead of towards it. This will basically demonstrate the probability that you can give your AI reactions to various stimuli. Perform the following:

1. We will get our **State** variable. Then, we want to subtract 1 from this, getting a 0 or 1 index. Next, we want to create a **Select** node and plug the results of the subtraction into the node.

2. From there, we want **Option 0** to be **1** and **Option 1** to be **-1**. This will make the character either Run or Flee from Target. Now, zoom in to the **Get Direction Vector** node.

3. Let's multiply **Return Value** by the **Get Direction Vector** node results. You must first convert Int to Float. Then, multiply this by the vector. Then, pull the vector back into **Make Rot from X**:

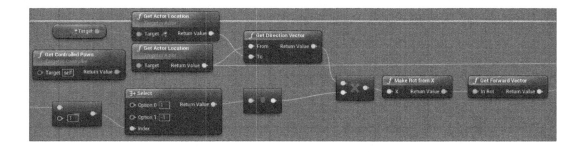

Back to the action

Let's focus back on Enemy EventGraph at the bottom. We want to implement a way for our AI to wander. Perform the following steps:

1. Start by searching for **Get Controlled Pawn**.

2. Next, we want to perform **Get Actor Location** on the controlled pawn. Then the vector it returns will be pinned to a Vector + Vector node.

3. From there, we want to create a **Random Unit Vector** node to generate a random vector from 0-1 on each individual axis.

4. We must pull from the **Stream** variable again and create **Random Float in Range from Stream**. Set the **Min** value to **-550** and **Max** to **550**. Then, we want to multiply what it returns by **Random Unit Vector**.

5. Lastly, the multiplied vector is added to the Vector + Vector node that we created in Step 2:

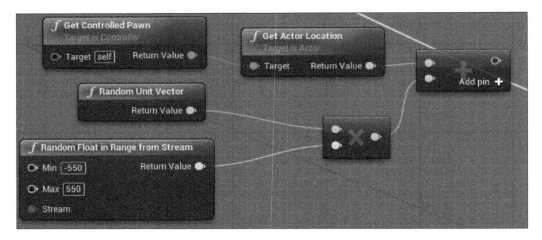

6. Now, we need to take the results of the Vector + Vector node and create a **Move to Location** node to instruct the possessed pawn to move to the **Move to Location** node of the vector.

7. We will take a look back at our first state, which checks for Actors within a radius. After **ForEachLoopWithBreak** is completed, we want it to execute **Move to Location**. So, pull from that and first create **DoOnce**.

8. We will do this because we don't want the bot to constantly be told to move to a location; we would rather have it do this after a random delay. So, now connect the **Completed** pin to **Move to Location**.

9. From there, we want to assign a new event. This event will reset **DoOnce** after the random delay. So, after **Event Begin Play**, we want to create **Assign MoveCompleted**.

10. From **RecieveMoveCompeted_Event**, create a **Delay** node. Pulling from the **Duration** node, we want to find **Random Float in Range from Stream**. We want to set the **Min** value to **2** and **Max** value to **5**.

11. After the **Delay** node is created, we want to connect this to the **DoOnce** node's **Reset** that we created in Step 7:

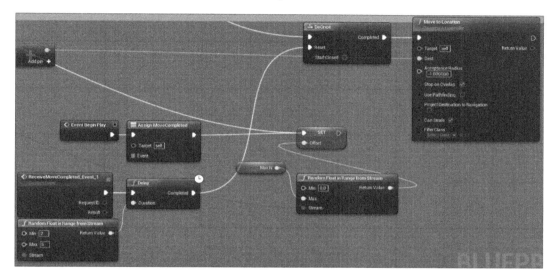

The results!

We should now be able to set the chance that our AI will flee. This probability script was made less predictable with the random variant offset for the probability range. We accomplished this by creating a Finite State Machine, which transitions between the necessary states at any given moment. So the scenario is that we are approaching the wandering AI, and once we are in range, the AI will either attack or flee. We have given it a 25% chance of fleeing by default. The AI flees, and the timer to reset the bot's state starts. Seconds later, the AI returns to the wandering state.

Summary

In this chapter, you learned about randomness and probability and how they are quantified. We used the tools within Unreal Engine to apply these theories. We understood this using a pseudo number generator, and we technically calculated randomness on a limited spectrum defined by the seed. We can use these non-uniform numbers to create probability functions, which tell the AI either to attack or flee. You also learned to create a FSM during the setup to create the states of the AI.

In the next chapter, we will explore the different techniques to introduce movement to our game's pawn. We will cover Path Finding, Navigation Mesh, EQS, and other related components that directly affect movement.

4
Introducing Movement

In this chapter, you will learn how to introduce movement into our AI characters within Unreal Engine 4. We will also go over the fundamental algorithms that allow us to instruct our characters to navigate to a point on a 2D plane. We will use other tools that will aid our AI in navigating the designated paths.

The topics that we will cover in this chapter include the following:

- Path Finding
- NavMesh
- Navigation and navigation modifier
- Blueprint navigation nodes

Overview

In this chapter, movement will be the main goal. How we achieve movement or use other tools to introduce movement are the questions we have to ask. Now that you're comfortable with some of the tools we use in AI, we have to make the AI capable of its most common action: movement. The system we use to introduce movement into AI is called Path Finding.

The way Path Finding works is by getting positions within the space designated as traversable. These start and end positions are fed to a function that computes the shortest path between the two positions. The algorithm uses relative position information, such as whether or not it is blocked by an object or actor, and prevents this position from being traversable. This is extremely useful when trying to generate a path in a world with dynamically moving objects.

Path Finding

We will break the operation of Path Finding into different components that all work cohesively. The first component is **NavMesh,** which represents the traversable path. This isn't the only Navigable Mesh generation component, but this is also the most commonly used representation of the Navigable Mesh. Another component is **NavMeshModifiers**, which can serve different purposes. A few examples are as follows:

- **Influence Mapping**: This allows you to feed the AI input information based on their location on NavMesh
- **Null Paths**: These simply allow you to cut out areas of NavMesh
- **Allowed Paths**: These simply allow you to block any AI that isn't allowed to navigate this area of NavMesh

The A* algorithm

At the core of the Path Finding system is an algorithm that calculates the shortest navigable path between two points on NavMesh. Dijkstra's algorithm is named after the computer scientist Edsger Dijstkra, who originally created it in 1956 and later published it in 1959 to find the shortest paths between two points. There are a few path finding algorithms worth mentioning, but the most commonly used in gaming is a variant of Dijkstra's algorithm. The variant is called the A* algorithm. A* works by having a list of traversable points. Then, from the start position, we want to search for the shortest path in each available direction. We can determine this by heuristic values. These values will tell us how much it costs to traverse to the next point based on some predefined rules. In A*, we traverse from a point to another point to reduce the exploration cost. The big difference between the two algorithms is the fact in A* that you have a heuristic value, which affects your pathing decisions. Heuristic values are obstacles to the predictive cost to travel to the next possible point. When the path is generated, we want the lowest heuristic value. So this means that by setting the heuristic values to 0, the algorithm is the same as Dijkstra's. Dijkstra's algorithm scans more nodes, usually making it less efficient because it doesn't predict the cost of traversing paths.

Let's take the following grid as an example:

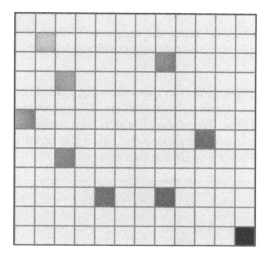

Dijkstra's algorithm takes every available point into account. So, in this example, we'll start from the upper-left corner and try to get to the lower-right corner, and all the adjacent nodes are considered to be connected and can be traversed from each other. Perform the following steps:

1. The algorithm scans all the available nodes, keeping a record of the shortest found path. Nodes with a different grayscale represent that the algorithm has to explore different locations to find the path:

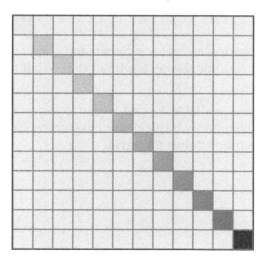

2. Once the goal is discovered, a trace back sequence is put in action, thus creating the path.

This can take a lot of steps, and that's the reason for which we adapted heuristics in A*. Instead of searching each node, we will continue from the shortest current path to the goal.

An example with A* is represented in the following grid. The algorithm will start from the first node (in the upper-left corner) and then scan the neighboring nodes to calculate the movement cost. The node at which the cost is the least is selected, and the nodes that are not selected are put on the list of the scanned nodes. This avoids us having to go to these nodes again for this query:

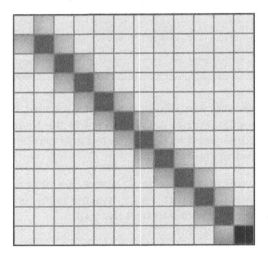

From step 1, the neighbouring nodes are scanned and checked for heuristic values or path cost to determine the next optimal step. What results is a direct path (if unobstructed).

There are other algorithms available, but A* is easy to implement and isn't resource-heavy, so it is commonly implemented in gaming engines as a way of creating paths between two points on a grid.

Navigation Mesh

Navigation Mesh in Unreal Engine 4 allows us to tell the engine where our traversable path should be generated, and we can optimize this to help generate more accurate paths for our AI. We will call Navigation Mesh "NavMesh" for short as most game developers are familiar with this term. If you're in Unreal Engine and you navigate to the **Modes** panel under **Volumes**, you'll see **NavMeshBoundsVolume**. This is a volume that you can use to cover the geometry and generate NavMesh on. I have a sample of what this would look like. If you can't see the green mesh generated by NavMesh, make sure you check the **Navigation** option (press *P* for shortcut) in the **Show** menu onscreen:

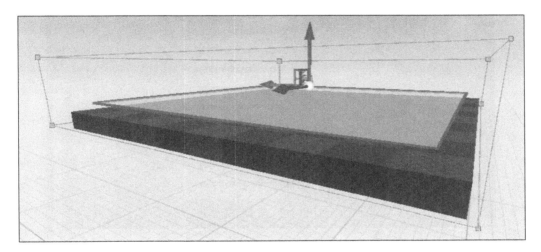

RecastNavMesh

On each level, you'll see a node within World Outliner called **RecastNavMesh-Default**. If you click on it, you can explore the default options that affect Navigation Mesh within the level.

If you go down to **Generation**, this is what you will begin to tweak according to your needs. If you're trying to get more performance when rebuilding at runtime, or precision with your agent's movement, try to optimize these values:

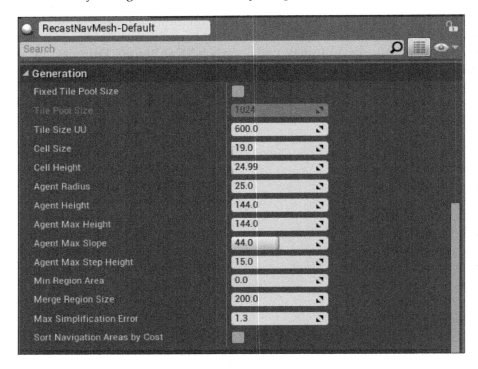

I will briefly go over some of the properties to give you an understanding of what role they play and how they affect performance. Let's look at some of the most important properties in **RecastNavMesh**:

- **Cell Size**: This is the 2D size of the voxel, basically a 3D pixel, which represents a space to navigate. This is the floor area of the voxel. This directly correlates to the resolution of NavMesh. Smaller sizes here generate more voxels, resulting in better movement precision. Unfortunately, performance takes a hit during the generation of NavMesh due to this.

- **Cell Height**: This is the height of the voxel. This value correlates to **Agent Max Step Height**, and it is suggested to be kept at half its value. NavMesh will not be generated if the **Cell Height** value isn't at least .1 less than that of **Agent Max Step Height**.

- **Tile Size UU**: When this is at lower values, it increases the NavMesh Generation performance. Try enabling **Draw Poly Edges** to see this in action.

- **Agent settings (Radius, Height, Max Height, Max Slope, Max Step Height)**: are specific to your agents and should be specified appropriately.

- **Min Region Area**: This gets rid of what looks to be artifacts of pieces of NavMesh Generation, which are too insignificant to navigate.

If you have any obstacles in your NavMesh and NavMesh is being generated on top the obstacles, then this object is treated as geometry, and for better performance, you can make your mesh be recognized as a Dynamic Obstacle. This prevents NavMesh from being generated on top of it. Now, to affect this area, you must set the **Offset** and **Extent** values for the **Box Collision** property as well. Take a look at the following screenshot:

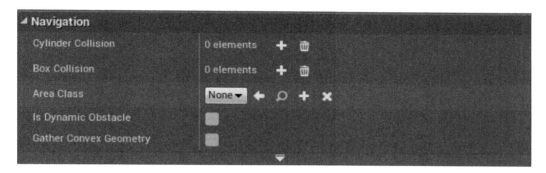

Let's walk through the steps:

1. Let's create a new **Box Collision** element. This will populate the array with an element containing two values.

2. We need to set the **Offset** value to the negative of half the width, length, and height of NavMesh. The **Offset** value is the position that the collision begins from.

3. Next, set our **Extent** value to half the width, length, and height of our NavMesh. The **Extent** value is how much it extends from the center point of NavMesh. This means that it correlates to half the volume size.

In this NavMesh, for example, I've set the properties accordingly; take a look:

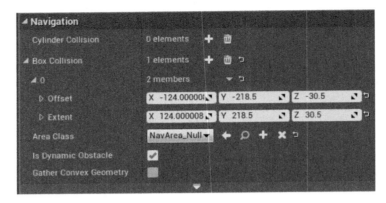

As you can see in-game in the following screenshot, the correct location is affected by the `NavArea Null` class we set on the **Is Dynamic Obstacle** option:

The movement component

The movement component is the driving force behind animation. Similar to the other types of movement components, such as a vehicle's movement component, we will provide inputs, which will then communicate with other components in the backend to properly simulate animation or gear ratio changes. What this means is that other functions can also influence the pawn that has the movement component. So, if our Behavior Tree tells the AIController to focus on another pawn, the AIController will influence the direction that the pawn it possesses is facing. This means wonders for not having to explicitly tell your pawn this information.

The AIController

We previously used the AIController to move our pawns in *Chapter 2, Creating Basic AI*, and *Chapter 3, Adding Randomness and Probability*, but never took the time to understand what's happening within Unreal Engine 4 to make it happen. Having this understanding allows you to expand on movement components when, for example, you want to create your special extensions of the movement component to support the receiving of instructions such as Move to Location for a vehicle.

The AIController is a controller specifically built for AI. Similar to the PlayerController, it controls the pawn it currently possesses. The main difference is that the AIController comes with functions, which allow you to move AI using tools such as Move to Location. With Move to Location, you can specify the Acceptance Radius value, whether or not to use Path Finding, and other useful options. There is also a simple version of Move to Location, which sometimes provides smoother movement at the cost of not able to change the options. This means that all the options are default, as shown in the Move to Location node.

It's called **Simple Move to Location** and is located as in the following screenshot:

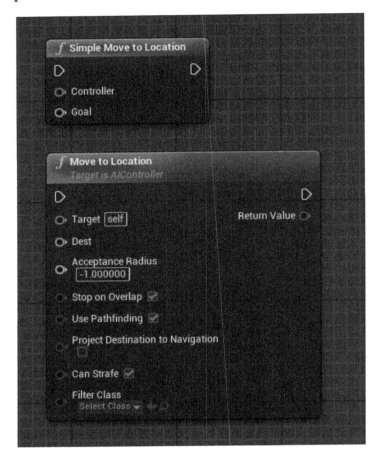

Let's start!

Open up Unreal Engine 4, and let's start a new **Third Person** template project. We want this so that we can use the Third Person pawn as one of our AI-controlled pawns. So, select the settings as in the following screenshot and hit **Create Project**:

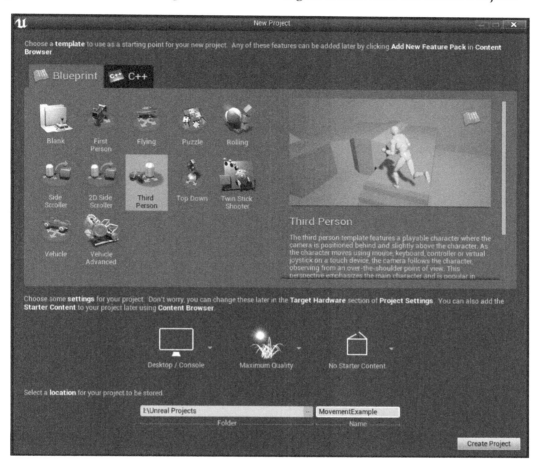

Next, we want to create our new AIController, and this will be responsible for telling our pawn to move between two points. The plan is to introduce some obstacles to see the effect we can have on the pathing of our AI. Perform the following steps:

1. Let's start by going into the **Blueprint** folder. Right-click to create a new AIController class and name it SoldierAI. This AIController will be responsible for navigating the pawn provided by the starter content.

2. Remove the pawn from the level initially set up by Content Example. Then, we want to place two new **ThirdPersonCharacter** pawns in the level across from each other. Next, we want to open up this **ThirdPersonCharacter** blueprint and access its default values.

3. From here, let's find this pawn's default AIController and change this value to our new AIController class named SoldierAI. What this will do is always spawn our pawn with our AIController:

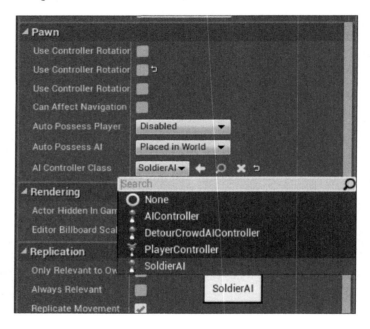

Save all! Let's proceed to the next part of this chapter!

Waypoints

In this chapter, waypoints represent the points that bots navigate to. We will make additional changes to our waypoints to limit who can traverse these points. This will be established by creating an array of actors on individual waypoints. When the pawns go to access the list of available waypoints, they will only add the waypoints they're allowed to. Here are the steps to perform for this:

1. Start in the same **Blueprint** folder as before. Right-click on it and create a new blueprint. Go to **Custom Classes** and select the **Target Point** actor. We will use this for the sprite it provides.

2. Name this new **Target Point** subclass `Waypoint` and hit **Okay**.

3. Open our new `Waypoint` custom blueprint and create a new public **ThirdPersonCharacter** pawn array variable called `Allowed Access`. Then, select **Editable** so that we can modify this value directly from Unreal Editor:

4. Now, place some waypoints in the world, and we want to try to make this random. This will allow our pawn's path to be more controlled when we go over some other topics later in the chapter.

5. I choose to place seven waypoints in my world and have them share about three of them to create some uniqueness in the paths. So, inside one of the nodes, let's add both of the available pawns that we placed in the world previously.

Navigation

Now that we have our soldiers in the world, we want to navigate them to their respective waypoints. This will be done through the AIController we set up on our soldier. If we focus again on Unreal Engine, we can get started! Follow these steps:

1. Open the AIController class we created earlier and named `SoliderAI`.

2. Then, we want to navigate to the **EventGraph** section. From there, we want our AIController to begin navigating to its first route as soon as it possesses a worthy pawn. So, let's add an event to drive this action (I encourage the use of events). The one we are looking for is called **Event On Possess**. This will also return the pawn it possessed, which we can use to compare with the `Allowed Access` list from waypoints.

3. Pull from the exec pin, and let's assign a new event called **RecieveMoveCompleted**. This event will continue the pawn to the next route as soon as it completes the previous one:

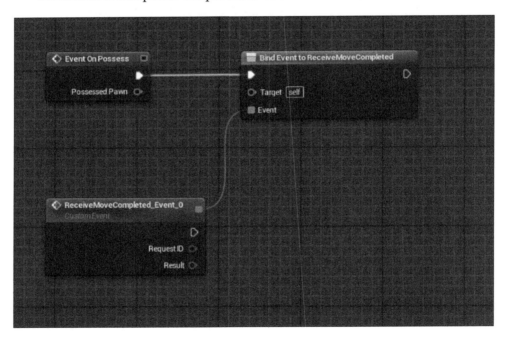

4. Now, after the **Bind Event** exec pin, let's put in **Do Once** to prevent this from being called twice.

5. Next, let's right-click, search for the **Get All Actors of Class** node, and select our custom blueprint called `Waypoints`. We want to now search through the available list of waypoints and check whether we're allowed to navigate there.

6. So, create a **ForEachLoop** node from the **Out Array of Actors** array and pull the **Allowed Access** array from **Array Element**. Then, we want to pull the pawn returned from the **Event On Possess** variable and cast it to the ThirdPersonCharacter pawn.

7. From there, let's try to find the pawn in the **Allowed Access** array. The array will return -1 if nothing is found, which means that we do not have access!

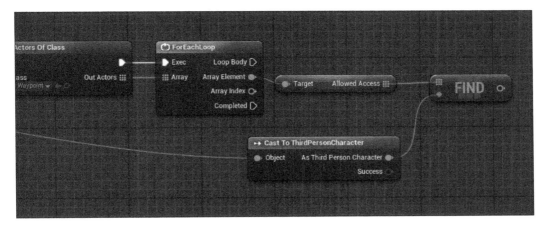

8. We need to pull a `Compare Int != Int Boolean` operation and compare our results from **Find** with -1. This will then be pumped into a **Branch** node.

9. Now, when this **Branch** node returns `True`, this means that we are allowed to navigate to the current **Array Element** pin, and we should add it to our points to navigate to.

10. Now, let's create a new **Routes** array on our pawn to hold the waypoints we can navigate. Then, we will pull this node to the **Branch** node we just created and pull **Add** from the array node. This will allow us to quickly access the routes we have assigned to us.

11. Now, we need to tell the pawn to navigate to the waypoint after this operation is completed. This can be done by pulling another **Routes** array out past the last nodes we placed.

12. We want to shuffle our **Routes** array so that our next destination is random. You can do this by pulling from the array and searching for **SHUFFLE**. This should be called last before our next operation:

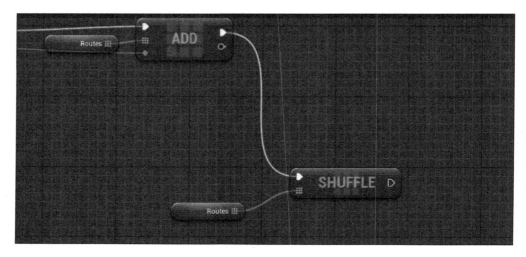

13. Next, we have the location that the pawn needs to go to, and we need to tell the pawn to move. We have two options: the first is to provide the **Move to Location** node with a location, and the second is to provide an actor and allow the engine to handle finding the destination. I will choose the latter for this example.

14. Right-click and search for the **Move to Actor** node, and we want to pump the first actor in the index from the **Routes** array we created earlier:

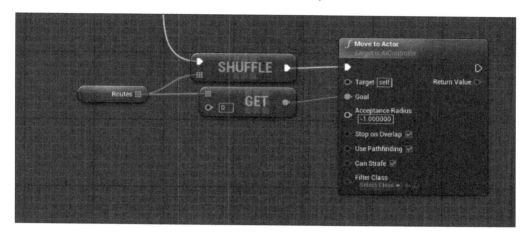

15. From there, let's track back to our **ReceiveMoveCompleted** event and pull from this to our **SHUFFLE** node. Now that this is completed, we want to go back to the editor. Let's simulate and see what AI does!

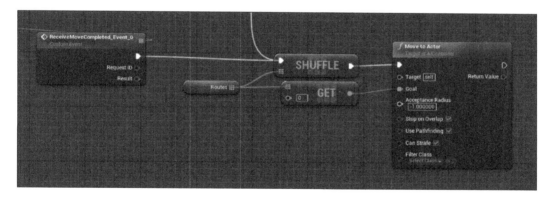

Now, let's get back!

Navigation Modifiers

Do you remember when we talked about heuristics? Navigation Modifiers allow you to directly affect the cost of navigating areas in which the modifier directly overlaps. You can also represent this affected area with a new color.

Now, in our example, we will analyze the behavior of AI as it traverses the different Navigation Modifiers we set up. What you want to understand from this is that heuristics help to find an optimal solution faster than Dijkstra's algorithm alone while utilizing the same method of discovery.

So, for example, if you have a cityscape and want your AI to stay on the sidewalks and out of the streets as much as possible, you could place Navigation Modifiers in the streets, which makes traversing the area highly costly. So, your AI will only ever traverse these areas if the appropriate path is blocked off by other high costs, such as obstacles.

Now, let's head to Unreal Engine 4 editor and get ready to create our own obstacles to see this behavior in action. We will also touch on **NavModifierVolume** and how you can use it in Unreal Engine 4.

Back in the editor

Let's navigate and look at the **Modes** window. In the first tab, we want to click on **Volumes**. Now, within **Volumes**, you'll see NavModifierVolume, and this will need to be dragged into the level:

1. Drag **Multiple NavModifierVolume** into the level. We want these volumes to block the direct paths between the waypoints we created earlier.

2. So, after dragging the volumes out, we should have some nice separation between **NavModifierVolume** and **Waypoints**. The screen should look similar to the following screenshot:

3. Next, we need to create **NavArea**, which will override the properties of the Navigation Mesh that **NavModifierVolume** overlaps.

The NavArea class

This class is responsible for applying the adjusted cost of NavModifierVolume. This also goes to say that NavModifierVolume is used to affect the Navigation Mesh. NavArea classes are used explicitly to override properties or functions in the affected Navigation Mesh. Today, we will create two NavArea classes to represent two different types of environmental situations. One will be the representation of water and the other, mud. The theory behind this is that water would have a high entry cost because it is not as fast as stepping in mud, but mud would have a low travel cost increase because it's not easy to walk in.

With this in mind, let's move on to the next step, which is creating different NavArea classes to apply to our NavModifierVolume actors:

1. Right click on our **Blueprint** folder within **Content Browser** and go to **Blueprint Class**.

2. From there, we want to go to **Custom Classes** at the bottom of the window.

3. Search for **NavArea**, and let's create a new subclass from this.

4. After creating one more **NavArea**, let's name one `AreaOfMud` and the other, `AreaOfWater`.

5. Double-click on `AreaOfMud`, and let's go to **Default Properties**.

6. In there, you will see **Default Cost** and **Fixed Area Entering Cost**.

7. We want the **Default Cost** value to be **2.5**, and this will affect the NavModifierVolume actor it belongs to.

8. For **Fixed Area Entering Cost**, we will leave this at **0.0** for mud. Lastly, change the **Draw Color** color to brown so that we know what's affecting the Navigation Mesh. As we stated earlier, entering mud is relatively easy in comparison to water:

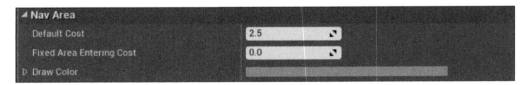

9. Let's close this and then open `AreaOfWater`.

10. We want to change **Default Cost** to **1.5**, and let's change **Fixed Area Entering Cost** to **35**. These values could be tuned according to the specific game you are working on. And of course, change **Draw Color** to something similar to light blue to represent water.

11. Save and close and then go back to the editor!

12. Now, let's go and apply these NavAreas to the NavModifierVolumes we placed on the level earlier.

13. Once you do that, you should now see **Draw Color** updated. Let's hit **Play** and now observe our AI!

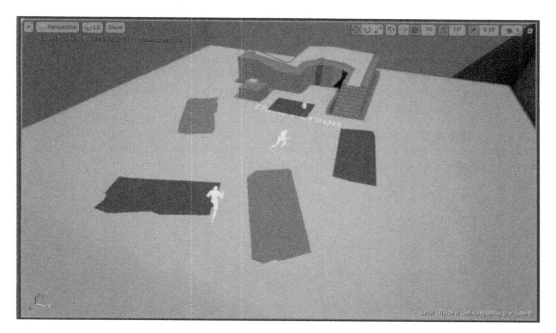

The navigation cost

As you can see, the AI does exactly as you predict. It avoids the mud because of the cost that is applied as it traverses NavModiferVolume, and sometimes, water's Fixed Area Entering Cost wards off the AI, although more than often, the AI is found traversing the water because once you're in, everything is okay! This was usually the trick for me. So, with this said, I hope you've understood the A* algorithm and its search to find the most optimal path.

Summary

In this chapter, we covered the different tools that allow us to control and influence the behavior of our AI's movement using NavModifierVolumes and other recast properties. We also learned how to tell our AI's controlled pawn to navigate to the waypoints that belonged to them. Lastly, we covered more fundamentals, such as the pathing algorithm originally created by Edsger Dijstkra. Next, we learned that we can optimize his original algorithm in favor of performance and resources and achieve this through heuristics.

In the next chapter, we will create a behavior tree and adapt what we've learned from the previous chapters to create some interesting AI interactions. We will also take advantage of the sensory system provided in Unreal Engine 4.

5
Giving AI Choices

In this chapter, you will learn how to introduce autonomous behavior into your characters using Behavior Tree. Behavior Tree is a methodology that allows you to view your AI logic visually. Behavior Tree is a type of hierarchical task network resulting in a state-oriented design. So, each state will dictate our current task instead of a goal.

This chapter will cover:

- Behavior Tree
- Blackboard
- The components of Behavior Tree, including Selector, Decorator, Service, and so on
- Building a Behavior Tree to run on a dog character

Behavior Tree in AIController

In this chapter, we will use Behavior Tree and scripts to create our autonomous state-oriented behavior. However, before we get to a higher-level control of our AI, let's understand some of the fundamental components of what allow us to control our AI. So, from the start, we have AIController, which is similar to PlayerController; this controller is responsible for interpreting all our AI input. This input is applied by the world when we request that it is moved.

With this in mind, we can introduce influence through multiple avenues within the code. We could tell AIController to move to a location, or we can tell AIController to run Behavior Tree. What's also very important to understand is that movement is applied with the CharacterMovement component. If you created a subclass from CharacterMovement, you can extend and continue to use the same Behavior Tree to introduce movement in theory.

One example of this is the car AI project I created for the Unreal Engine 4 development forums.

The link for the same is `https://forums.unrealengine.com/showthread.php?25073-UPDATED-5-16-A-I-Templates-Bot-Car-amp-Flying-AI`.

The internal movement component was responsible for taking the Move To request from the Behavior Tree. So, this allowed me to tell my car to go to certain locations, know when it was finished, and simply repeat the process. This is powerful if you're trying to create AI because a majority of what you need to do is move.

Creating Behavior Tree

Moving onto Behavior Trees, let's begin to construct our first tree! In this project, we will create AI that resembles the behavior of a neighborhood dog. It will change its behavior state randomly every so often and continue to search for any mailman, who may loiter by its dog pin.

This will touch on using **Environment Query System** (**EQS**), which is still an experimental but powerful feature in Unreal Engine 4. It will be responsible for handing the dog a new position to search for the mailman in. So, if you're ready, let's open up a new Third Person project.

Let's create a few things for our dog to route between. The following are the steps to do so:

1. First, let's make a new custom **Target Point** class and name it `Foodbowl`.

2. Next, let's make a new custom **Target Point** class and name it `DogHouse`:

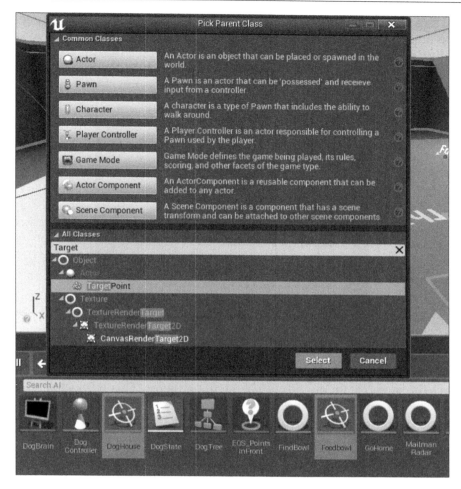

3. Place these two actors accordingly within the world. We will use these to reference our dog where to move to when in the appropriate state. So, basically, we will use Target Points or waypoints to reference the vector location of this actor within the blueprints later on.

4. Now, we need a new Enumeration class called DogState; this will hold our current state of the dog. This value is important for executing the correct tree for the appropriate responses we send to the AI, such as detecting the nearby mailman.

5. The `DogState` class will have `Hungry`, `Barking`, and `Idle` as the three available states. `Hungry` will be responsible for telling the dog to navigate to the dog bowl to eat food. The `Barking` state will tell the dog to search for the mailman. The `Idle` state will tell the dog to go to its dog house. At any time, the dog will begin to chase the mailman if he gets too close:

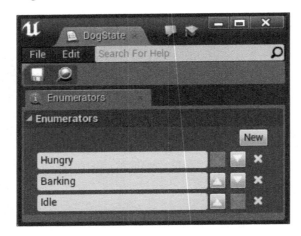

Blackboard

This stores the memory for an individual agent or agents. This works hand in hand with the Behavior Tree. It allows easy and direct access to variables from any of your Task nodes. Imagine that your Behavior Tree is your EventGraph, and Blackboard is your variable that you use in EventGraph. With the **Instance Synced** function, you can replicate the variable to every instance of the Blackboard class within the world. Now, let's start creating our Blackboard:

1. We need to create a new Blackboard (which is under AI assets when you right-click within **Content Browser**) and name it `DogBrain`. This will store our **State** as Enum `DogState` for the Behavior Tree branches, `Mailman` as **ThirdPersonCharacter** if we have one found, `Foodbowl` as itself if we have found, and lastly our latest search `Locations` as a vector for EQS. You may see the elements we created as follows:

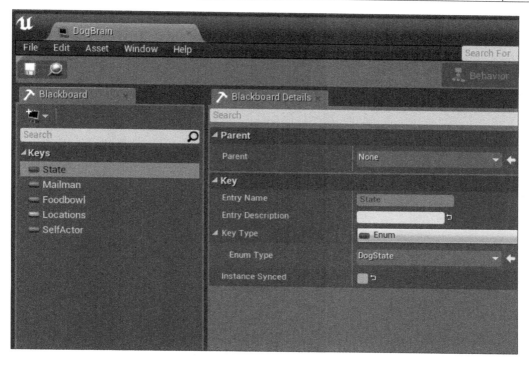

2. Let's save this all. We have to create Behavior Tree now that we have the bare components that make up our Behavior Tree. Let's go over these quickly:

   ° `DogState`: This will store our current state because this is a state-oriented tree

   ° `DogHouse`: This will represent where our dog house is located for the dog to sleep

   ° `Foodbowl`: Similar to `DogHouse`, this will be the location of the food bowl when the dog is hungry

Designing Behavior Tree

Let's name our Behavior Tree `DogTree` and make sure our `DogBrain` Blackboard asset is plugged into the **ROOT** entry node. The Blackboard asset set here has variables that can be accessed by the functions within the tree during execution. When variables are instanced and synced, you have a global variable for `Mailman` that all other dogs with the same Blackboard asset can see.

Our Behavior Tree will be set up in visually similar way to the following screenshot:

What you can note here is that we will start with a **Selector** node. This is because we do not want to exit the tree if our child node fails. If it fails, we want to continue to the next node that will ultimately succeed. Within individual trees, we will do something different. Now that we are in a state, we sometimes want to control the sequence of events in order to replicate a particular behavior for this state. So, for our Hungry state, we will first need to have a bowl. Once we have our bowl, we can go eat. We will also include a waiting node, and this makes our dog seem like it's searching for its dog bowl. This happens only the first time. Next time the condition check to the bowl being set will be true, and we will immediately move to our Foodbowl.

In our Barking state, we will immediately go into a **Selector** node because we want to again execute whichever tasks there are and wait till one succeeds. This means the task in which the condition is met returning successful and resulting in failure for a **Selector Composite** node. For this, we need to execute a few functions, and all must return success.

This is important to understand because this basic logic is what allows you to construct a desired execution behavior in Behavior Tree. So, in the following breakdown, I will outline the process in the order of execution and how the construction of the tree depends on the direction of the flow of execution:

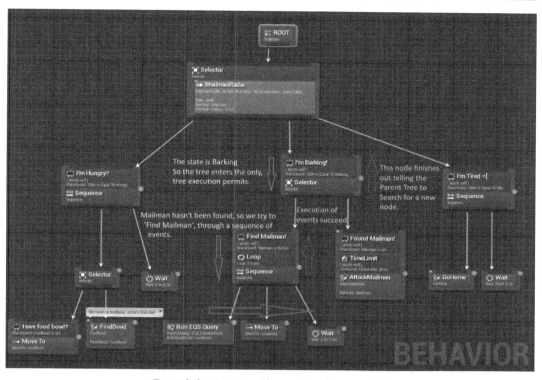

Target behavior tree with execution flow overlaid

The **Tree Search** event is within **Service** named **MailmanRadar**, and we will use this event to move the transition states.

Lastly, we have our `Idle` state, which simply makes the dog return to the dog house.

So with this, let's continue the preparation for our dog AI. We now need to create an AIController for our dog, and this is because the AIController is responsible for executing Behavior Tree. We will simply perform the following steps:

1. So, let's create a new blueprint and select **Custom Classes**. Then, we will search for `AI Controller`.
2. Now, we can name it `DogController` and create it!
3. We also need to create **Service**, which will determine which state to be in. To do this, right-click and create a new blueprint. Under **Custom Classes**, we need to search for `BTService_BlueprintBase`. Let's name it `MailmanRadar`.

The Behavior Tree service

What makes this node unique is that it is designed to run and monitor the branch it is attached to. It will execute at its defined frequency to make checks and update the Blackboard as long as its branch is executed. Today, we will utilize these functions. The first **Event Receive Activation** node notifies us that the **Branch** node is activated, and this is perfect for initializing variables within the Blackboard related to this branch. The next node we will use is **Event Receive Search Start**, and this notifies us when a branch is being chosen. We will take advantage of this and change our state, which tells our tree to choose a new path of execution. The following screenshot shows the overall blueprint for **MailmanRadar** service:

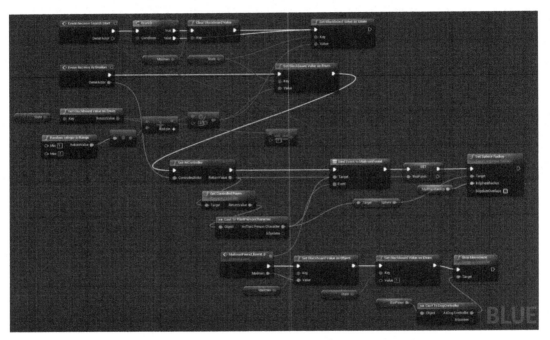

Overall blueprint for Mailman radar service

Now, for our radar to work, we have to set up the equipment on the pawn. It will be responsible for relaying information to Behavior Tree whenever another pawn overlaps it. So, let's find our ThirdPersonCharacter and open it up!

1. We need to go to **Viewport** and create a new **Sphere Collision** component. This component sphere radius will be updated by our radar function within the tree.

2. Now, let's add the **OnComponentBeginOverlap** event in EventGraph.

3. Let's create **Event Dispatcher** by adding in the **My Blueprint** pane. Drag it to EventGraph and select **Call**. This **Event Dispatcher** will be responsible for notifying the tree of changes. Let's name this event `MailmanFound` and give it an input type of **ThirdPersonCharacter** named `Mailman`.

4. From our **Overlap** event, we will cast **Other Actor** to ThirdPersonCharacter, call `MailmanFound`, and supply the casted actor:

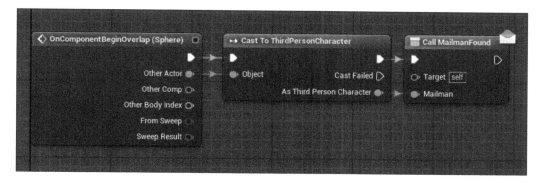

5. Now, let's head to `MailmanRadar` and set up some other variables to respond to this event. We need to add a few variables to hold references while this radar scans for possible mailman targets:

   ° First, we need a Blackboard Key Selector variable named `State`, which is editable

   ° Next, we need a Blackboard Key Selector variable named `Mailman`, which is also editable

   ° Next, we need a Float variable named `MailmanRadius`, which is editable and has a default value of 512

   ° Lastly, we need to create a type Actor variable and call it `thisPawn`

   The screen should look like the following screenshot:

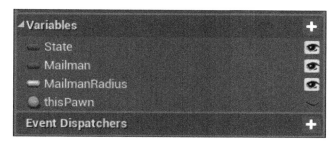

6. Start with our initializing event, **Event Receive Activation**.

7. We will use this to initialize our Blackboard variables. So, let's get our **State** variable so that we can set the initial state.

8. Pulling from the **Get State** variable, we want to find **Set Blackboard Value as Enum**. Get state from the variables, and this time, we want **Get Blackboard Value as Enum**. We will choose a new random state for our AI. We will do this by incrementing our **State** variable randomly once or twice. So, let's pull from this, create Byte + Byte, and then create a modulo (%). This modulo will take our results from the addition (+) node, but we want **3** to be put in the last position. So, we will have something similar to *Input % 3 = Range (0-2)* (which translates to Hungry, Barking, and Idle).

9. Now, let's create **Random Integer in Range** and set the **Min** value to **1** and the **Max** value to **2**. Then, we want to pump this into the Byte + Byte addition node. The **False** value from our previous **Branch** node will pin into our **Set Blackboard Value as Enum** node.

10. Lastly, pin the results of our modulo (%) to our **Set Blackboard Value as Enum** node to update our current **State** variable:

The screen should look like the following screenshot:

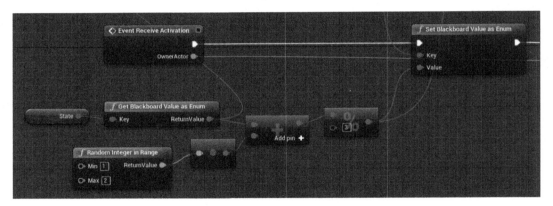

State transitions

What we will do here is randomly increment our state forward. This simply demonstrates the state transition. This operation is important because how you handle transitions can create virtually coherent AI. This is established when you have goal-oriented AI. Instead of being purely reactive, it actively chooses the best scored state to achieve said goal. This makes it seem as though AI has a level of intelligence.

Our AI randomly chooses its next state, but if the AI could make its new state decision based on the information we collected, it would make our AI appear intelligent. These examples will provide you with the knowledge to take on more challenging projects:

1. Looking back at **Event Receive Activation**, let's pull **Get AIController** from **Owner Actor**. Then, we want to pull **Get Controlled Pawn** in order to assign the **Event Dispatcher** node we created earlier.

2. Cast the **Get Controlled Pawn** node to ThirdPersonCharacter, and from the cast, assign **MailmanFound**.

3. We also want to take **Owner Actor** and set it in our **thisPawn** variable. Lastly, we should update our pawn's **Sphere** variable to match our variable node's **Radius**, which we want to check for:

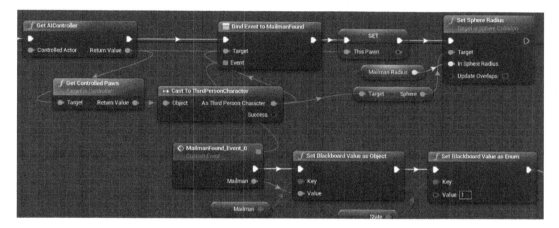

4. From our newly created **MailmanFound** event, we want to set our **Mailman** Blackboard selector. So, get it from variables, execute **Set Blackboard Value as Object**, and set **Value** from **Mailman** returned through the event.

5. Next, set our **State** variable to `Barking` so that we immediately abort other states and continue with `Barking`. Get the **State** variable from the variables and **Set Blackboard Value as Enum** node. We want to make this value **1**, which represents our `Barking` state.

6. Lastly, let's get our **This Pawn** variable from our variables node. Cast this node using **Cast To DogController** and then call **Stop Movement**. This will stop any current movement and begin the next requested movement:

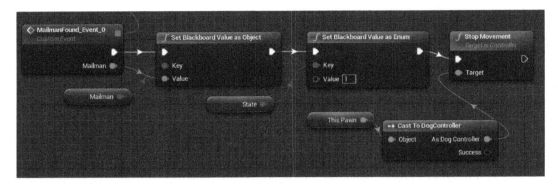

7. Now, with **Event Receive Search Start**, the tree will look for a new branch to begin. So, we will use this to set the new states. So, right-click on our graph and pull the event out. From here, we want to pull out the **get State** variable from the side, and while pulling from our pin, find **Get Blackboard Value as Enum**.

8. From here, we need to create an equal to 1 condition and then connect it to a **Branch** node. What we did by comparing the state to **1** is that we said our **State** variable is equal to Barking, allowing us to perform specific operations to leave this state. This branch will be the next executed node.

9. Now, we need to pull our variable, **Mailman**, and call a function to reset the values of our Blackboard Key. We will do this by pulling from the **Mailman** pin and searching for **Clear Blackboard Value**. This will be called if the **Branch** node we created returns **true**.

10. We also want to set a new state if we get our **State** variable and pull **Set Blackboard Value as Enum**. We can update our current **State** variable using the calculation we made on **Event Receive Activation**. So, pull from this modulo (%) and set it to **Value** for our **Set Blackboard Value as Enum** node:

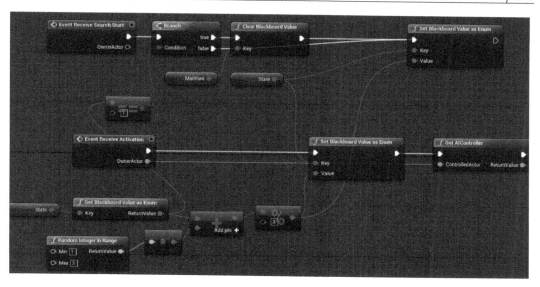

11. Let's open this `DogController` class and find the **Event Begin Play** node.

12. Right-click on the graph and find the **Run Behavior Tree** node.

13. Then, in the **BTAsset** pin, let's find **DogTree**, which we created earlier. Then, in the game, we will assign our **DogController** class to our character. This will spawn with the character and immediately run **DogTree**:

14. Back to our Behavior Tree, let's pull down an arrow and create a new **Selector** composite in our graph. This is the start in the tree shown in the preceding screenshot. It will run our patented **MailmanRadar Service** node. What is unique about **Service** nodes is that they're used on composites only and are responsible for handling tasks that require running with the tree.

15. For now, let's construct the next three node options in the tree. This will be three sequence nodes with Blackboards Compare Decorators on them. Decorators can apply conditions to our Composites or Task nodes. These decorators will check for the appropriate entry state to begin the execution.

16. So, create our Composite node from the beginning of this tree. Then, let's right-click on this node and add a Decorator that we want to look for in the Blackboard:

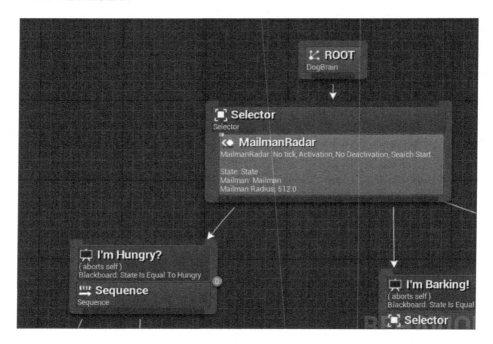

Blackboard Compare Decorator

There are a few fields we want to take notice of in the pane:

- Let's start with **Flow Control**. This has two properties: **Notify Observer** and **Observer aborts**. **Notify Observer** tells **Flow Control** which operation to fire on. The **On Result Change** fires when the computed condition to enter this tree changes. So, if we were barking originally but are now idle, the tree's **Flow Control** will fire off an **Abort** event. Which part of the tree is aborted is controlled by **Observer aborts**. The first option is **Self**. This is straightforward in that it aborts further execution within this tree. The second option is **Low Priority**. This option basically says the rest of the tree will be aborted. This is good if you want the whole tree to start over. The last option is simply a combination of the first two options I mentioned.

- The next field is **Blackboard**, and this is responsible for telling the Decorator which condition returns **True**. In this instance, we want to set the **Blackboard Key** to **State**. Note the properties change. Change the **Key Query** value to the condition we apply to the **Key** value. Then lastly, set the **Key** value to the value we are checking our condition on.

Let's go back to our Behavior Tree:

1. The first node in the Sequence branch is a **Selector** node. We want this behavior because we have two conditions that we want to be checked for, but we know that only one condition can be met at a time. The next node we need to create within this Sequence branch is a **Wait** node. This will simulate our dog finding or animating while it sniffs out or eats its food.

2. The first node within our **Selector** node is the node responsible for moving to our bowl assuming we have it, using **Move To**. The **Move To** node takes one Blackboard Key argument, and this is compatible with Actors or Vectors. This provides a limited but direct way to execute movement from the tree:

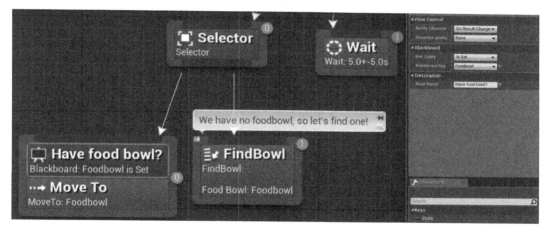

3. The next node within our **Selector** node needs to be created. So, let's go back to our Content Browser, and create a new Blueprint. Under **Custom Classes**, we want to search for **BT**, and we will create **BTTask Blueprint Base**. This will be called **FindBowl**, and it will be responsible for finding the food bowl for our dog.

4. We will now save this new asset, go back to our dog tree under our **Selector** node, and create our new **FindBowl** task after the **Move To** node. We have now said that this node will execute if other child conditions, such as **Foodbowl**, is set as **false**.

5. Now that we have our first State tree, we should update the comment on our tree nodes to understand what it means in shorthand. Look at how I've done in mine in the following screenshot:

6. Now moving onto the next tree, we must create a similar setup, starting with a **Selector** composite node. We want to right-click, add a Decorator, and search for **Blackboard**. This needs to check whether the **State** variable is equal to `Barking` to execute this branch entry.

7. Next, we will create a **Sequence** Composite node responsible for telling our AI to sniff around for the mailman. This will have a Blackboard Decorator on the composite to check if the **Mailman** variable is set. We also want to add another **Loop** Decorator responsible for calling this twice if the condition is met.

8. With this set, the next three nodes within this **Sequence** branch will first scan the area, move our dog, and then wait at the location sniffing. So, in order to scan our area, I want to use **EQS (Environment Query System)**.

Environment Query System

I want to cover this more in the next chapter, which covers how our AI can sense the environment, but I will at least introduce the idea and how we will use it today. Environment Query System is responsible for allowing the context object to call a query request to generate information based on filters and the test applied to the request. A query would contain a template of instructions for EQS to run. So, for example, if you want to scan an area for possible hiding places, you can scan for those actors that represent the hiding places. Then, you can apply filters to your query to get rid of the results you don't want to score and score your results based on direction from enemy for the most optimal hiding position.

In our case, we want to choose a strategic position to sniff out our Mailman. We will do this by creating Environment Query. Let's create this as follows, and in our next chapter, we will cover other ways of using EQS:

1. So, with this in mind, let's head to the Content Browser and select our **AI** folder. Right-click on the folder and go to **Misc** and then to **Environment Query**. Name it `EQS_PointsAround`.

2. Let's open this and go to root. In here, you'll notice a similar visual interface to that of Behavior Tree. Pull from the root and find **SimpleGrid**. This will generate a grid of items around our actor to be scored and returned to the requester.

3. We want to change the **Grid Size** value to 2048 and that of **Space Between** to 512. The rest of the settings will be default; let's now add a test as shown in the following screenshot:

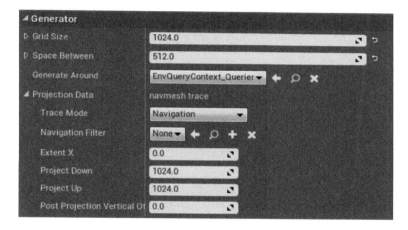

4. This test will filter and then score our results based on the direction from our dog. In order to determine the DOT test to score, we have to tell the test what we want to have tested. So, **Line A** will be our item's **Rotation**. **Line B** will be the direction between us and the item.

5. Lastly, as our dog will need to search the whole area, we would need our dog to have the opportunity to survey the whole area. By enabling **Absolute Value**, we are able to get the results to score in both directions.

6. We want to adjust our filter to eliminate items directly in front of us or to our right by choosing a range in between 0 and 1. Let's change our **Filter Type** value to **Range**, the **Float Value Min** value to **0.4**, and the **Float Value Max** value to **0.85**.

7. The last thing here is **Score**, and we will leave this as the default. Let's save this and go back to our Behavior Tree:

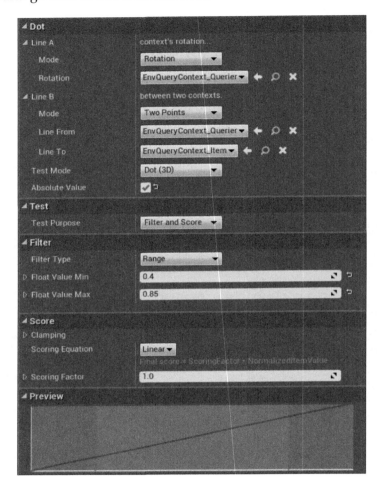

8. From the **Sequence** node we created with the **Mailman is NotSet** Decorator, we want to now run our EQS query and store the results in our **Location** Blackboard key. We can pull from the node and find **Run EQS Query**.

9. Then, we need to select our **EQS_PointsAround** option and set our **Location** Blackboard key.

10. The next node will move our dog to the location returned by EQS. Let's pull and find **Move To**. This Blackboard key needs to be our location.

11. The last node here will make our dog wait at the newly found location for a random amount of seconds. So, find the **Wait** node, and let's set the **Wait Time** value to **2.5** and that of **Random Deviation** to **5.0**. The complete structure for the **Selector** nodes is shown here:

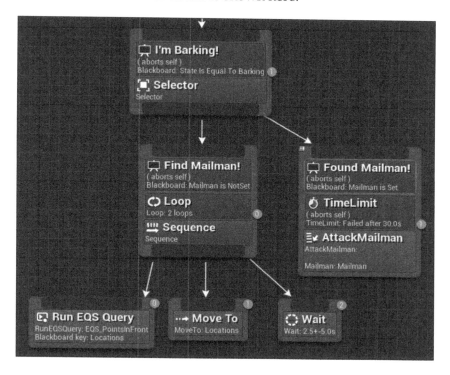

12. Back in our **I'm Barking** node, we will create a new node that will make our dog chase the mailman once the variable is set. We must first create our own node, which will never finish execution. So, let's head to the Content Browser.

13. We must go in our **AI** folder, right-click, and create a new blueprint. Under **Custom Classes**, we have to find the **Task Blueprint Base** Behavior Tree. This will be named `AttackMailman`.

14. Let's open this up and head to EventGraph. First, we need to pull our location, so we must first create a reference to our Blackboard asset. Under **Variables**, create a new **Selector** Blackboard key and name it `Mailman`. This will need to be editable.

15. We have to find **Event Receive Execute**, and this will open up **Gate**. So, create a **Gate** node and pump our event into the **Open** exec pin of our **Gate** node.

16. We then need to create **Event Receive Tick** and pump it into the **Enter** exec pin of the **Gate** node. Then, we need to pull **OwnerActor** from the **Event Receive Tick** exec pin and cast it using **Cast to DogController**. From here, we can tell our DogController to **MoveToLocation**.

17. Now, we must provide a location. Pulling our **Mailman** variable, we must next pull **Get Blackboard Value as Object**. Then this will be cast to our ThirdPersonCharacter. From here, we can get our **Mailman** actor's location and tell our dog to move to this location:

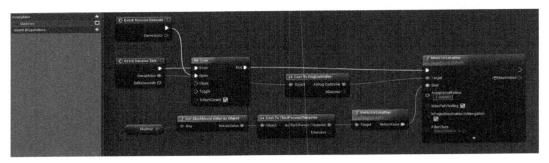

18. Last the **Idle** sequence will simply represent when the dog is tired and wants rest. Starting from the main branch, we will create a new state tree using a **Sequence** Composite node. We must right-click on our **Sequence** node and add a Blackboard Decorator. This will check whether the current **State** value is equal to **Idle**.

19. Pulling from our main branch, let's create a **Sequence** node. This node will have a Blackboard Decorator, which will have **State** set as the **Blackboard Key** value, and the **Key Query** will be set to **Is Equal To**. Our Blackboard **Key Value** for the decorator should be **Idle**.

20. Under **Flow Control**, we should make sure that the **Notify Observer** value is **On Result Change** and the **Observer aborts** value is **Self**.

21. Update our **Description** field to **Idle/Sleep** state to make our tree easier to understand:

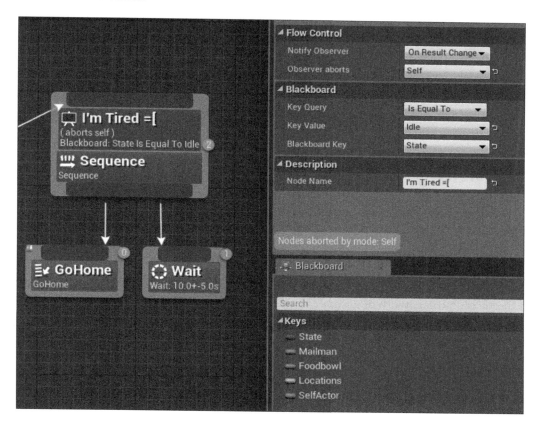

22. We need a new tree that will send our dog home and make it wait there.

23. Let's head to our Content Browser and navigate to our **AI** folder. Right-click and create a new blueprint class. This will be another custom class under **BTTask_BlueprintBase**. Name this GoHome, and open this up to EventGraph.

24. The event we want is **Event Receive Execute**, and this will call **Get All Actors of Class**.

25. The Actor class should be **Dog House**, and we will only have one in a level. **Get All Actors of Class** returns **OutActors**; get the first index item from this array.

26. Let's cast **Owner Actor** from our **Event Receive Execute** to **DogController** and then execute **Move To Actor**.

27. The last thing we want to call is **Finish Execute** and return **bSuccess** as true:

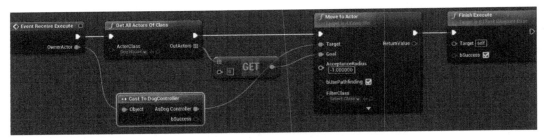

Summary

This chapter was definitely heavier with instruction, and so will it be the following chapters. In this chapter, we exposed how we can effectively make our AI reactive to other pawns and also how to move to different target locations. We also used EQS briefly to help our dog choose strategic sniffing locations. In the next chapter, you can expect to use EQS further. Though the detection is event-based, the movement is still done by the tree.

In the next chapter, we will go over the components built within Unreal Engine 4 that sense other AI and can help us achieve more flexible and responsive AI.

6
How Does Our AI Sense?

In this chapter, you will learn how to use the different components available within Unreal Engine 4 to enable our AI to sense the other AI and pawns that we place within the world. We will do this by taking advantage of a system within Unreal Engine called AI Perception components. These components can be customized and even scripted to introduce new behavior by extending the current sensing interface.

The topics we will cover in this chapter are as follows:

- AI components
- Registering a perceivable actor using AIPerceptionStimuliSource
- Perceiving objects using AI Perception
- The state machine

Overview

AI Perception is a system within Unreal Engine 4 that allows sources to register their senses to create stimuli, and then the other listeners are periodically updated as the sense stimuli is created within the system. This works wonders for creating a reusable system that can react to an array of customizable sensors. So, this chapter will focus on using the AI Perception component to have our enemy AI chase us whenever we are detected. What we will do differently is that this will all be scripted using Blueprint. So, there is no need to use Behavior Tree this time around!

AI Sense

Let's start by bringing up Unreal Engine 4 and open our **New Project** window. Then, perform the following steps:

1. First, name our new project `AI Sense` and hit **create project**.

   After it finishes loading, we want to start by creating a new AIController that will be responsible for sending our AI the appropriate instructions.

2. Let's navigate to the **Blueprint** folder and create a new AIController class, naming it `EnemyPatrol`.

3. Now, to assign `EnemyPatrol`, we need to place a pawn into the world then assign the controller to it.

4. After placing the pawn, click on the **Details** tab within the editor. Next, we want to search for **AI Controller**. By default, it is the parent class **AI Controller**, but we want this to be `EnemyPatrol`:

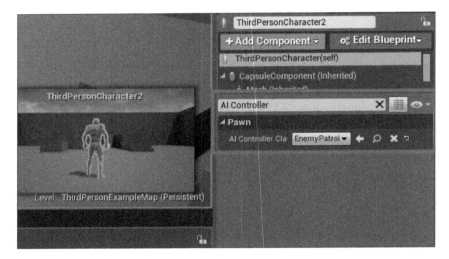

5. Next, we will create a new PlayerController named `PlayerSense`.

6. Then, we need to introduce the AI Perception component to those who we want to be seen by or to see. Let's open the `PlayerSense` controller first and then add the necessary components.

AI Perception components

There are two components that are currently available. The first one is what you're already familiar with: the AI Perception component. The other is the AIPerceptionStimuliSource component. The latter is used to easily register the pawn as a source of stimuli, allowing it to be detected by other AI Perception components. This comes in handy, particularly in our case. Now, follow these steps:

1. With **PlayerSense** open, let's add a new component called **AIPerceptionStimuliSource**. Then, under the **Details** tab, let's select **Auto Register as Source**.

2. Next, we want to add new senses to create a source for. So, looking at **Register as Source for Senses**, there is an **AISense** array.

3. Populate this array with the **AISense_Sight** blueprint in order to be detected by sight by other AI Perception components. You will note that there are also other senses to choose from — for example, **AISense_Hearing**, **AISense_Touch**, and so on.

The complete settings are shown in the following screenshot:

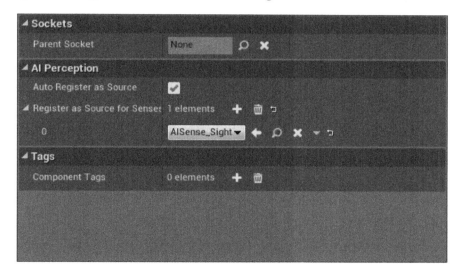

This was pretty straightforward considering our next process. This allows our player pawn to be detected by Enemy AI whenever we get within their sense's configured range.

Next, let's open our `EnemyPatrol` class and add the other **AI Perception** components to our AI. This component is called **AIPerception** and contains many other configurations, allowing you to customize and tailor the AI for different scenarios:

1. Clicking on the **AI Perception** component, you will notice that under the **AI** section, everything is grayed out. This is because we have configurations specific to each sense. This also goes if you create your own AI Sense classes.

2. Let's focus on two sections within this component: the first is the **AI Perception** settings, and the other is the event provided with this component:

   1. The **AI Perception** section should look similar to the same section on **AIPerceptionStimuliSource**. The differences are that you have to register your senses, and you can also specify a dominant sense. The dominant sense takes precedence of other senses determined in the same location.

   2. Let's look at the **Senses** configuration and add a new element. This will populate the array with a new sense configuration, which you can then modify.

3. For now, let's select the **AI Sight** configuration, and then we can leave the default values as the same. In the game, we are able to visualize the configurations, allowing us to have more control over our senses.

4. There is another configuration that allows you to specify affiliation, but at the time of writing this, these options aren't available.

5. When you click on **Detection by Affiliation**, you must select **Detect Neutrals** to detect any pawn with **Sight Sense Source**.

6. Next, we need to be able to notify our AI of a new target. We will do this by utilizing the Event we saw as part of the **AI Perception** component. By navigating there, we can see an event called **OnPerceptionUpdated**.

This will be updated when there are changes in the sensory state which makes the tracking of senses easy and straightforward. Let's move toward the **OnPerceptionUpdated** event and perform the following:

1. Click on **OnPerceptionUpdated** and create it within the EventGraph. Now, within the EventGraph, whenever this event is called, changes will be made to the senses, and it will return the available sensed actors, as shown in the following screenshot:

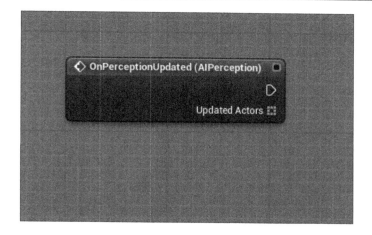

Now that we understand how we will obtain our referenced sensed actors, we should create a way for our pawn to maintain different states of being similar to what we would do in Behavior Tree.

2. Let's first establish a home location for our pawn to run to when the player is no longer detected by the AI.

   In the same **Blueprint** folder, we will create a subclass of **Target Point**. Let's name this `Waypoint` and place it at an appropriate location within the world.

3. Now, we need to open this `Waypoint` subclass and create additional variables to maintain traversable routes. We can do this by defining the next waypoint within a waypoint, allowing us to create what programmers call a linked list. This results in the AI being able to continuously move to the next available route after reaching the destination of its current route.

4. With `Waypoint` open, add a new variable named `NextWaypoint` and make the type of this be the same as that of the `Waypoint` class we created.

5. Navigate back to our Content Browser.

6. Now, within our `EnemyPatrol` AIController, let's focus on **Event Begin** in EventGraph. We have to grab the reference to the waypoint we created earlier and store it within our AIController.

7. So, let's create a new waypoint variable type and name it `CurrentPoint`.

8. Now, on **Event Begin Play**, the first thing we need is the AIController, which is the self -reference for this EventGraph because we are in the AIController class.

9. So, let's grab our self-reference and check whether it is valid. Safety first! Next, we will get our AIController from our self-reference. Then, again for safety, let's check whether our AIController is valid.

10. Next, we want to create a **Get all Actors Of Class** node and set the Actor class to `Waypoint`.

11. Now, we need to convert a few instructions into a macro because we will use the instructions throughout the project. So, let's select the nodes shown as follows and hit **convert to macro**. Lastly, rename this variable **getAIController**. You can see the final nodes in the following screenshot:

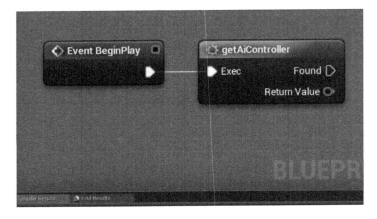

12. Next, we want our AI to grab a random new route and set it as a new variable. So, let's first get the length of the array of actors returned. Then, we want to subtract 1 from this length, and this will give us the range of our array.

13. From there, we want to pull from **Subtract** and **get Random Integer**. Then, from our array, we want to get the **Get** node and pump our **Random Integer** node into the index to retrieve.

14. Next, pull the returned available variable from the **Get** node and promote it to a local variable. This will automatically create the type dragged from the pin, and we want to rename this `Current Point` to understand why this variable exists.

15. Then, from our **getAIController** macro, we want to assign the **ReceiveMoveCompleted** event. This is done so that when our AI successfully moves to the next route, we can update the information and tell our AI to move to the next route.

State machines

Traditionally, we would default to the AI Behavior Tree, which is available to anyone using UE4. However, in our scenario, we will break the job of Behavior Tree into components directly written in blueprint. So, the next thing we need to create is a way to maintain a state. Then, we can essentially create a state machine by updating the variable, allowing our AI to transition into different states by controlling the execution flow.

We will establish this using an event that will update our state when the conditions we specify are met. To start this off, let's continue to the next step!

1. First, let's create a new Int variable in our AIController called **State**. This will maintain our current state within our state machine.

2. We now need a new event, and we will call it **NextRoute**. So, upon right-clicking on the event graph and going under **Add Event**, we will notice **Add New Event**. Let's name this new event `NextRoute`.

3. Now, after our assigned event **ReceiveMoveCompleted,** we should call **NextRoute** to initiate or enter the state machine:

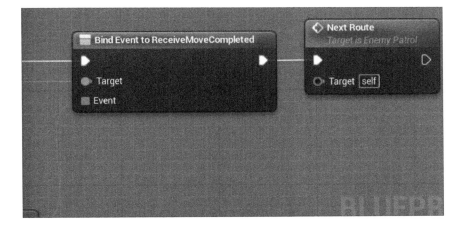

4. Next, focusing on **ReceiveMoveCompleted**, let's switch on **Result**. From the switch node, let's pull **Success**. This means that only when the move is completed by our AI will we continue on to the next step in the execution flow.

5. From **Success**, let's create a new **Branch** node and set up a new condition. This condition will check whether our **State** Int variable currently equals **0**. The value **0** represents our default state.

6. If our **State** variable's value is **0**, let's create a **Retriggable Delay** node and set it at **0.2** seconds. Next, we want to check whether our **Current Point** variable is valid; if so, we want to grab the variable we created earlier to define the next route in the linked list.

7. From there, we want to set this new variable into our **Current Point** variable. This will allow us to indefinitely navigate between waypoints.

8. Next, we want to create two new variables that will be responsible for delaying the amount of time till we continue to the next route.

9. So, let's create a new Float variable called **RoutePauseDelay**, which will define how long we will wait. Next, we want to create deviations so that the wait time isn't always the same. So, now create a new Float variable called **RoutePauseDevia**.

10. Let's pump **RoutePauseDeviation** into **Random Float** in **Range** and add this to **RoutePauseDelay**. Then, this will be pumped into a **Delay** node.

11. From the **Delay** node, we want to call the **NextRoute** event, which we created earlier.

12. Focusing on the newly created **NextRoute** event, let's check whether our **State** variable is equal to **0** and create a **Branch** node to check the results when executed:

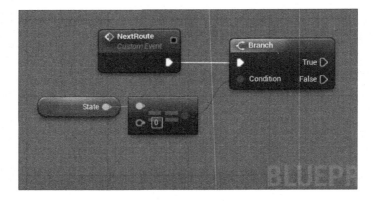

13. Next, we should get our AIController from our Actor, and check whether our **Current Point** variable is valid.

14. Next, if our **Current Point** variable is valid, then we should pull from **Return Value** of the **getAIController** and **Move to Actor** nodes.

15. From there, pull the **Current Point** variable we checked and put this into the goal of the node. Now, when the AIController takes possession of the actor it belongs to, it will call this event. Once the move is completed, it will update the route and continue to the next route.

Pawn detection

To give our pawn the most up-to-date information, we need to create an event that will catch and respond to the sensory update events from the AI Perception component. We will establish this by creating a new event that is solely responsible for processing detected pawns. Here are the steps:

1. Let's right-click anywhere and go under **Add Event**. From there, we want to add a custom event, and we will name the new event `Detected Enemies`. We have to also create a new actor array parameter named `Detected Actors` to hold the array of **Updated Actors**.

2. Now, in the next step, we need to recompile a blueprint to call the AIController and the **Detected Enemies** function from our **OnPerceptionUpdated** event:

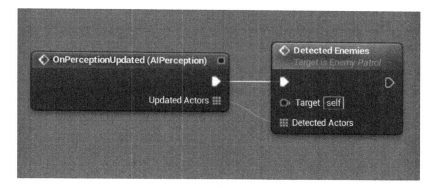

3. In the next steps, we will handle the transitions between different states. For example, we can be in the default state and find a new enemy. From there, we need to stop the current movement and move toward the detected enemy. If we lose sight of an enemy that we've been chasing for a specific amount of time, we can cancel the movement and go back to navigating our waypoints.

4. Now, we want to focus again on the **DetectedEnemies** event we created earlier. Now that this event is called by our AI Perception component, we want to use these actors appropriately for each state.

5. Let's pull from this event and create a **Branch** node. Next, we want to create the condition for this branch. We need to pull our **State** variable and check whether it equals **0**. If it is **True**, we will check whether we detected any enemies.

6. So, pull from **True**; let's check whether the length of our **Detected Actors** array is longer than or equal to **1**. If it is, we have enemies, and we can move forward in the process. So, pull from **True** of the previous **Branch** node and then create a new branch. This will check for the length of the **Detected Actor** array.

7. Next, if we found an Enemy, we will change the state to change the execution path. We can do this by setting the **State** variable as **1**:

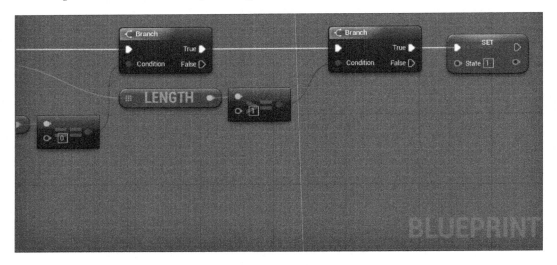

8. Next, we create a new switch statement for our **State** variable. This will help us with the execution flow. We want the start of the index to begin from 1 and have no default pin.

9. Now, we can backtrack to our first **Branch** condition, where we will check whether the state is equal to **0**. Then, when this statement is **False** — meaning we're currently in a state of searching for our enemy — we would want this to lead to the switch statement as well. This will allow our state to transition out of the state if we've lost the enemy at some point.

10. Focusing on the switch node, let's add another break for index 2. Then, pulling from one, let's call **GetAiController**. If **Found** is executed, then we're ready to move forward.

11. Let's pull the **Detected Actors** parameters from our event and create a **ForEachLoopWithBreak** node. From this node, let's check whether the enemy detected is within sight. Right-click and search for **Line of Sight To**, keeping **Target** to self. Then, **Other** should be the **ArrayElement** variable.

12. Pulling from **Return Value**, we will create a new **Branch** node. This branch condition will need to check whether we have **Current Enemy**; if not, we will set a new enemy. From the **True** value of the **Branch** node, let's set an Enemy actor from **Array Element**.

13. Pulling from **GetAiController**, we want to set focus on the enemy we just set in Enemy actor.

14. Next, we want to get our AIController again and create the **Move To Actor** node. Then, we will set the Enemy actor to our goal for the node. This will navigate our AI to our new found enemy.

15. Next, let's switch on **Return Value** from the **Move To Actor** node. We will get a node that switches on **Failed, Already At Goal**, and **Request Successful**. Let's pull from **Request Successful** and set our **State** variable to **2**.

16. From our **Set State** variable, we want to then break our **ForEachLoopWithBreak** node. This way, we won't continue to search for enemies once we find them:

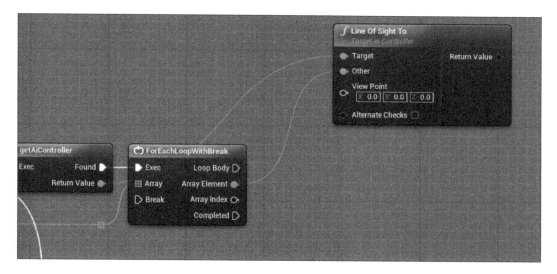

17. Let's go back in our loop at our first **Branch** node, and from **False**, we will create another branch. This will check whether the **Array Element** pin, our enemy that we just selected **Line Of Sight To** for that failed, is the enemy we currently have targeted. If so, we want clear to our **Enemy Actor** variable, and focus and set our **State** value back to **0**.

State transition

This concludes what is necessary for our transition out of state 1. Next, we will do what is required for state 2, and this will allow us to detect the changes necessary to exit this state back to state 0 once we no longer see the enemy. Perform the following steps:

1. Going back to the switch node on **State**, which we created earlier (in Step 55) and creating a new connection from 2, let's create **GetAiController**.

2. Next, we need to check whether our **Enemy Actor** variable is valid. We will do this by dropping out the **Enemy Actor** variable, pulling from the pin, and then creating the **IsValid** node.

3. If the variable is valid, we want to move our AIController toward our enemy. We can do this by pulling from **Return Value** on **GetAiController** and then creating **Move To Actor**. Then, we can connect our valid **Enemy Actor** variable to our **Move To Actor** goal input.

4. Next, we want to use the Tick event within the AIController to check whether we have the line of sight of our enemy when we're in state 2. We can do this by focusing on the Tick event, pulling from it and then creating a **Branch** node.

5. Then, drop the **State** variable and check whether it equals **2**. The results of this equal node are pumped into the condition of the **Branch** node.

6. Looking at the **Branch** node, pull from **True** and create the **getAiController** node. Then, we will pull from **Found** and create a **Branch** node.

   Now, we need to create two new variables to maintain the chasing of our enemy. This will allow us to either timeout our chase after a designated amount of time or have the chase end immediately, forcing the AI to return to routing between the waypoints we created.

7. So, let's create a new variable called **TimeoutChase**; this will be a Boolean. Next, create a **ChaseTime** variable, and this will be a Float. This will tell our execution line to switch between different flows if we don't want to timeout our chase.

8. Focusing again on the last **Branch** node we created, we want to plug in our newly created **Timeout Chase** variable into the condition.

9. If this **Branch** node is **False**, we want to plug it into the **getAiController** node from our previous switch statement. It should look similar to the following screenshot:

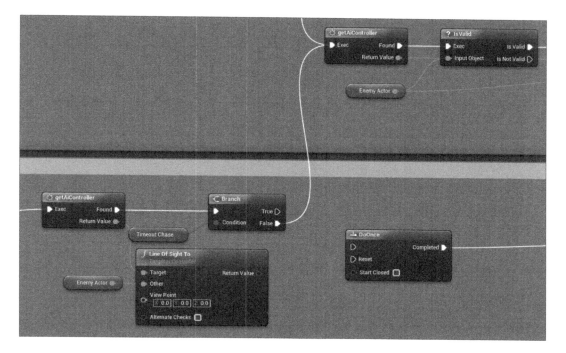

10. Now, if the statement is **True**, we want to create a new **Branch** node to check whether our enemy is in the line of sight. Pulling from **Return Value** of the **getAiController** node, let's create a new node called **Line Of Sight**.

11. Then, grabbing our **Enemy Actor** variable, we will plug this into our other input. Then, from the return value, we can create a new **Branch** node with the condition already set.

Resetting the state

Now, this next part will allow us to use our **ChaseTime** Float variable in a **Retriggerable Delay** node. Basically, when they're in the line of sight, the **Retriggerable Delay** node will continue to be reset. Once we lose the line of sight, the other execution path will execute **DoOnce**, attempting to reset our AI's **State** variable. Once the **Retriggerable Delay** node finishes delaying by the designated **Chase Time** value, it will reset **DoOnce**, allowing our bot to reset its state. Perform the following steps:

1. Now let's look at the **Branch** node we just created and pull from **False** and create a new **DoOnce** node. We can leave **Start Closed** as default.

2. If we track back to **True** from the previous **Branch** node, we can pull from **True** then create a **Sequence** node.

3. Pull from the first **Then 0** exec pin and create a **Retriggerable Delay** node. Next, let's plug in our **Chase Time** variable into the **Duration** variable. Lastly, let's plug in **Completed** into the **Reset** input execution of the **DoOnce** node we created earlier:

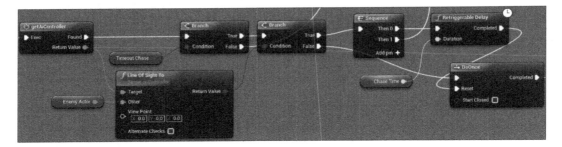

4. Back to the **Sequence** node, we need to route **Then 1** to our previous **Move To Actor** node, as we did in *State transition* section.

   So, while we see our enemy, we will continue to move toward them until we lose our Enemy, in which case it will switch to the other execution line. Now, if you want the AI to move toward the positions that the enemy was located at, you would need to get the actor's location and do so. This would result in having the AI move toward the last known position of its enemy before ultimately being reset.

5. Now, focusing on the **DoOnce** node, let's pull from the **getAiController** node we created earlier in the chain. Then, create a new node after the **DoOnce** node called **Stop Movement**. This will cancel any movement toward our enemy.

6. Next, we need to set the **Enemy Actor** variable to **null**. We will set our **State** variable to **0**. We will lastly call our **Next Route** event. Forcing the AI to return the routing between our waypoint once again, we will wait for an enemy to come in sight.

Simulating and playing

Now if we hit **Play**, we should see the AI chase you until you've broken sight!

So, the bot will route as it did previously until an enemy is within sight. If the bot is in state 0, it will enter state 1 once an enemy is detected by the AI Perception component. Next, if one of these enemies is within sight and we have no current enemy, we will change our state to 2 and set our enemy. Lastly, we will continue to move toward our enemy until we lose sight of them, resulting in us being set back to state 0. The following diagram illustrates these transitions:

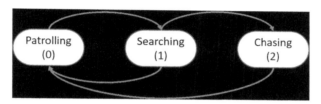

This is how we create AI without the assistance of Behavior Tree. Ultimately, you still need to create a state machine because this is the fundamental approach used in programming to create functions that transition among each other based on the variables shared by the functions. By doing this directly in blueprint, we can get a deeper understanding of the behavior-control mechanism based on state transition, and this is good for simple AI behavior.

Summary

This concludes the chapter on what you were to learn about the AI Sense component. This tool is great to easily integrate new responsive sensors to your AI's input, which you do not have to create yourself from things such as Ray Traces.

Next, we will focus on more advanced movement, such as getting our AI to avoid obstacles using some tools provided by Unreal Engine and also how we can have our AI follow one another, similar to the behavior in squads.

7
More Advanced Movement

In this chapter, we will focus on flocking and more advanced path-following behaviors. What we will try to achieve is implementing flocking behaviors to create realistic movement for our AI, such as when you need agents to avoid each other while all are moving in the same direction. Sometimes, it's necessary for your agents to seek a leader, so you can create different formations of agents. First, we want to set up everything we need to get some pawns moving around within a level. Next, we will add some blueprints to these pawns to give them the ability to discover new leaders. Lastly, we will introduce flocking behavior so that we can see how our AI moves as a group.

The topics covered in this chapter are as follows:

* Setting up an actor blueprint for movement
* Implementing following behavior
* Implementing flocking behavior with features such as separation, cohesion, and alignment
* Adding behavior control through UMG

Setting up the agents

Let's create a new project called AdvancedMovement using the Physics Ball template. Currently, we are using Unreal Engine 4.8.3. The first thing we want to do is find our PhysicsBallBP class and open up EventGraph. We can do this by implementing the points given as follows:

1. After our project is loaded, navigate into the **RollingBP** section and then into the **Blueprints** folder.
2. In here, you'll find PhysicsBallBP, and this will act as our agent in this chapter. Let's open up to EventGraph for this actor.

We want to introduce two new vector variables to hold the current direction of the agent. The other will hold the location where the agent is spawned.

3. Now, let's remove any unnecessary logic from the example. I removed the following variables:

    ○ The **JumpImpulse** variable

    ○ The **CanJump** variable

All the blueprint code located in EventGraph is not in the following screenshot:

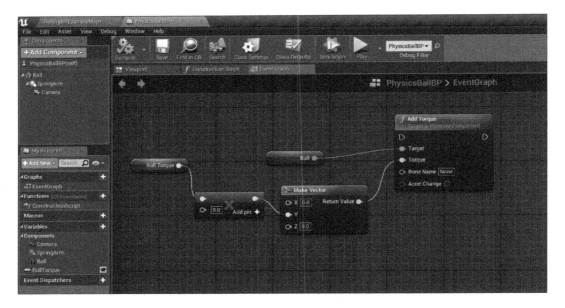

4. Okay, now that we have a starting ground, let's create a variable called **Direction** and give it the vector variable type.

5. Next, create a variable called **StartLocation** and set it as a vector variable type as well.

 StartLocation will be used later in the course for the **Reset** button we have to implement.

6. Now, find **Event Begin Play**, and let's initialize our new vector variables. First, right-click the area near the event and find **Random Unit Vector**. Split the vector (by right-clicking on the pin) from the **Random Unit Vector** node because we only want the **X** and **Y** values.

> We can only go forward or back and to the left or right. These deltas are handled by X and Y. If Z is introduced, it can potentially rotate the camera forward, which may be undesirable for viewing.

7. Next, let's right-click and create a new node called **Get Actor Location**. We have to pull down the **StartLocation** vector set variable. Then, from **Return Value**, set our **Start Location** variable. Comment the **Give random direction and save start location** area:

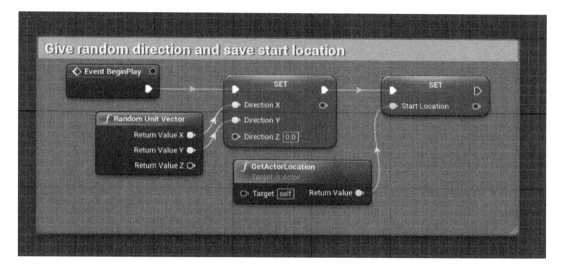

8. Now, we need to set the **Direction** variable to be the direction of the **SpringArm** variable. The reason for this is so that the camera always faces the direction in which we are moving in the world. So, when you modify the different variables, you can see it take effect.

9. Pull our **SpringArm** variable into EventGraph. Next, pull from the **SetRelativeRotation** variable.

10. We want to then get our **SpringArm** variable's current **RelativeRotation** value to interpolate it between the directions we should be facing. This creates a smooth transition when updating the camera's rotation.

11. By pulling from the **SpringArm** variable's current **RelativeRotation** pin, we want to create the **RInterp To** node.

12. Next, we want to get our **Direction** variable and convert this direction to a rotation using **Make Rot from X**.

13. We will change this rotator by an offset. I calculated this as the local rotation offset of the spring. With the direction in **A**, we should set **B** to have **0.0** Roll, **45.0** Pitch, and **90.0** Yaw.

14. Now, connect the **Return Value** pin to the **Target** pin of our **RInterp To** node.

15. Now, right-click, search for **Get World Delta Seconds**, and plug this into the **Delta Time** pin on our **RInterp To** node.

16. The **Return Value** pin must now be plugged into **New Rotation** for the **SetRelativeRotation** node we created earlier.

[So, we want to update our direction here. The reason for this is that we will continue to add to this operation to normalize our direction and get a value in the range we expect.]

Comment this area **Calculate Direction for Camera Spring Arm**:

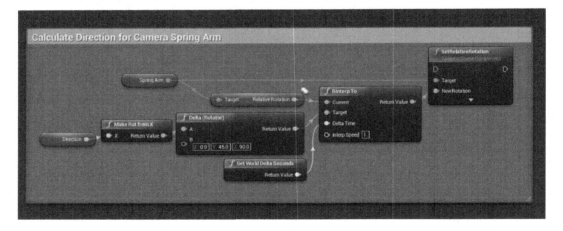

17. So, to do this, let's pull our **Direction** variable down. Pull from the variable and find Vector + Vector. From here, we want to normalize the vector. Lastly, let's break the vector.

18. Next, let's pull the **Direction** variable and create a set variable. Let's split the **Direction** set variable using **Break Vector**. Then, plug both **X** and **Y** float variables into the **Direction X** and **Direction Y** variables of the **SET** node.

Comment this area **Calculate Direction**:

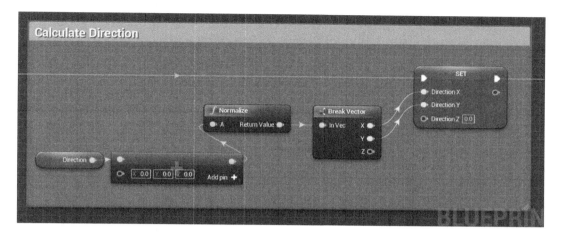

19. We need to pull a **Ball** variable and call a node named **Add Torque**.

20. To calculate the **Torque** value, we want to take the **Direction** variable. Get the **Roll Torque** variable and multiply it by the **Direction** vector. The results of this should be plugged into the **Torque** pin of the **Add Torque** node.

Comment this area **Apply Torque to Ball**:

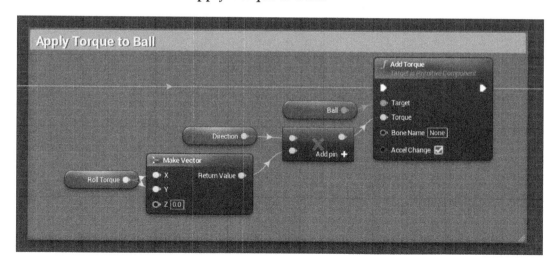

21. The next step is creating a function that will scan in front of the **Ball** variable. If a trace is hit, it means that we hit a wall. From here, we want to use **Hit Result** to generate a reflection off the wall based on **Hit Normal**. Let's see this in practice.

22. From our last node, let's create a new node called **LineTraceByChannel**. From here, we want get a new node by right-clicking and searching for **Get Actor Location**. Plug in **Return Value** into the **Start** pin of our newly created node.

23. Grab another copy of our **Direction** variable and place it in the graph. Pull from our **Direction** vector and right-click for a new node called **Make Rot from Y**. From **Return Value** of **Make Rot from Y**, right-click for a new node called **Get Up Vector**.

24. Get a variable for our **Ball** vector and then right-click for a new node called **Get LocalBounds**. Now, split the Max vector and from **Max X**, right-click for a new node, Float * Float.

25. Now, this variable will take our size and use it to determine a distance forward that is outside the sphere. In our example, we will scale by **-3.5**. We will invert our scale because the vector we will multiply is relative to the ball, not the world.

26. In the Float * Float node, let's make the other float **-3.5**, which is not connected.

27. From our **Get Up Vector** node, let's multiply it by the Float * Float result from the earlier step. Now, we need to right-click and find a Vector + Vector node. Add this vector to our **GetActorLocation** node. Then, plug the results into the **End** pin of our **LineTraceByChannel** node:

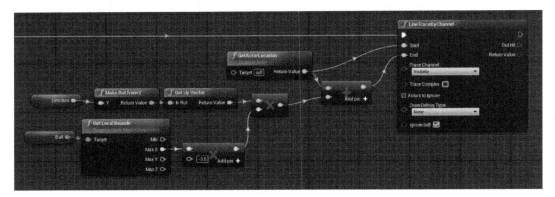

28. From our **LineTraceByChannel** node, split hit result. Now, find **Out Hit Blocking Hit** and create a branch from the Boolean result. Let's pull our **Direction** vector and get the **SET** variable. This should be connected with the **True** output pin of the **Branch** node created previously.

29. From our **Out Hit Normal** pin, right-click and create a **Make Rot from Y** node. Now, we want to pull from this return, right-click, and create a **Get Up Vector** node. This takes the normal from the world to relative direction space. Lastly, we want to get the **Direction** vector to get the variable.

30. Pull from our **Direction** variable and release to find **Mirror Vector by Normal**. Let's plug in the **Get Up Vector** node from the earlier step into **In Normal** of **Mirror Vector by Normal**. The results of this node are pinned to the **Direction** pin of the **SET** variable executed on the **True** statement.

Comment this area **Bounce current direction off wall cloding in front of ball**:

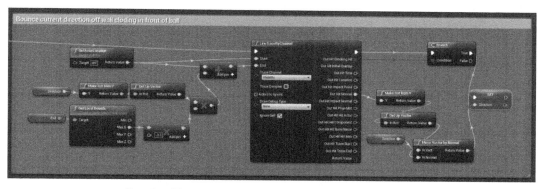

Complete blueprint setup for Bounce current direction off wall

Now that our `PhysicsBallBP` class or agent is updated to handle the direction vector, we will initialize it with random values. It should perpetually move forward and bounce off walls as the actor gets close enough to the impact.

Viewing the agent

We want to hit **Play** and make sure our agent bounces off walls. Once you hit **Play**, it should play, and the pawn you spawn with will go perpetually forward. We will then mirror the direction by normal once collision has occurred:

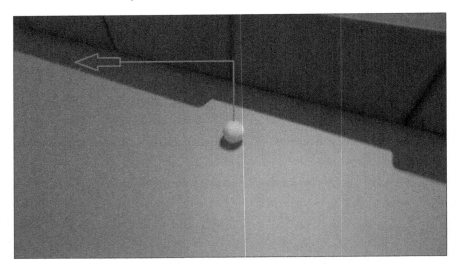

Following the agent

We want our Agent to follow its leader agent in whichever direction it goes. While still following the other logic to bounce off walls and the movement behavior we plan to introduce, we will create an example showing how this will affect the agent's movement as follows:

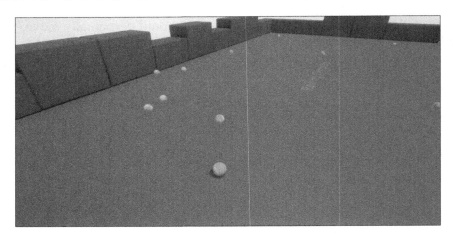

This step requires us to create a few variables and one function. We want to hold our Follower and Leader actors when operating in a free setup. We also need `LeaderDirection` to hold the direction that the agent should be moving in. Lastly, we can mark agents to be followers or leaders by enabling or disabling a Boolean called `isLeader`.

With these variables, we can keep track and prevent leaders from following followers, which can create interesting movement behavior but not what we intend to make happen in this demonstration.

Follow or lead

Let's open our `FlockingBall BP` class and view EventGraph. Find where we will update our **RelativeRotation** pin for our **Spring Arm** variable. Between this and **Calculate Direction**, we will add this new set of instructions:

1. First, we need to reference any actor near our agent. We can do this by the **SphereOverlapActors** node. Right-click on the graph and search for this.

2. Now, let's get the **Get Actor Location** node. Right-click, find this, and plug it into **Sphere Pos** of the node we created in the previous step. Next, set the **Sphere Radius** value to **300**. Now, let's pull from **Object Types** and create the **Make Array** node. So, we should populate **Object Types** with **Physics Body**. Next, we want to set our **Actor Class Filter** node to **Flocking Ball** to prevent unwanted results. Lastly, create another **Make Array** node, right-click on the graph, and search for it. Then, populate the first element with a reference to **Self**. Then, plug this array into actors to ignore. Comment this area **Search for nearby FlockingBalls**.

3. Now, let's focus on the **Out Actors** array. Right–click on the graph and search for **For Each Loop**. Let's pull from **Array Element** and cast this to FlockingBall.

   We have to know whether the agent we attempt to follow is following us. Otherwise, we can experience unwanted movement behavior.

4. From the **Casting** variable, let's find the **Leader** variable and compare it to **Self** with equal (==). Take the **Condition** pin and create a **Branch** node. If it is **False**, we need to check now whether we are Leader, and if we have either Leader or Follower.

   Before we move on, comment this branch with **Don't follow, followers as leader**:

5. So, search for the **isLeader** variable and create this variable. Next, search for **Leader** and check whether it is valid by creating the **Is Valid** node (which is a function). We have to do the same thing for another variable called **Follower**.

6. Now, connect all three Boolean conditions into an **OR** node. This will return **True** if any of our conditions return **True**. If any of these conditions return **True**, they're already following an agent or leading another agent:

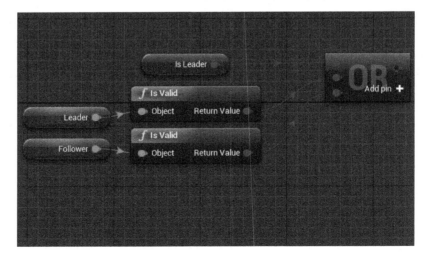

7. From this **OR** node, let's search for a new **Branch** node and connect it to the **Condition** pin. Now, if this **Branch** node value is **False**, let's create a node called **IsValid** (macro). The object we want to check is the casting we made in step 3. Pull this and create a reroute node near the **IsValid** (macro) node so that it can be used by other nodes easily.

8. If **IsValid** (macro) returns **Is Valid**, we want to create a **Branch** node. We want to check two conditions to be **True** with an **AND** logic gate in this statement.

9. First, let's get the **Leader** variable from the reroute. Then, we will compare it to **Self** with not equal (**!=**). Create an **AND** logic gate and connect the first pin to the results of the not equal (**!=**) condition.

10. Next, let's grab the **Follower** variable from the reroute. Then, compare this node using equal (**==**). Next, connect this to the **AND** logic gate in the previous step.

11. Lastly, connect this **AND** logic gate to the **Branch** node. If this node returns **True**, then let's set the **Follower** pin from the reroute. Plug in a reference to **Self** into the **Follower** pin. Then, set the local **Leader** variable from reroute.

Comment this area **If we don't have a leader, and we are not one. Find one**:

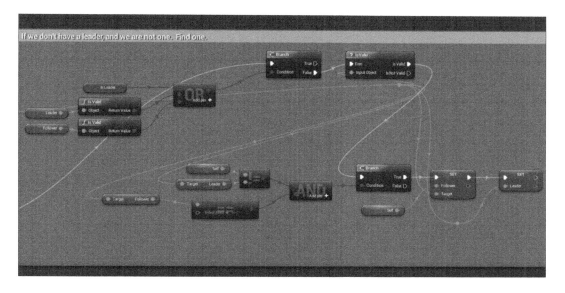

12. Now, go to the **Completed** pin of the **For Each Loop** node. Let's create a local **Leader** variable and check whether it is valid using **Is Valid** (which is a function). Now, create a **Branch** node and plug in the **Condition** pin from the prior node.

13. If the **Branch** node returns **False**, we want to set the **Leader Direction** value of the **SET** variable to **0.0**, **0.0**, and **0.0**. If our **Branch** node returns **True**, we want to calculate the direction toward our **Leader** variable.

14. Create a new node called **GetActorLocation**, and from the return, we will create **Get Direction Vector**. Now, let's right–click on the graph and search for the local **Leader** variable. Then, create the **GetActorLocation** node from the **Leader** variable and plug this into the **To** pin of **Get Direction Vector**.

15. From the **Get Direction Vector** node, pull **Return Value** and create **Make Rot from Y**. Next, we want to create **Get Up Vector** from the previous rotation. Then, from **Return Value**, this will go into **Leader Direction** of the **SET** variable.

16. Both **Leader Direction** local variables will lead to area commented as **Calculating Direction**. We must also go to **Calculate Direction** and add **Leader Direction** to the final direction calculation.

    Comment this area **Calculate Leader Direction**:

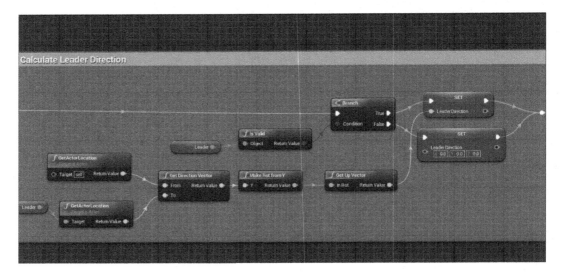

 Now, if we hit **Play**, we can see what happens. Little groups that begin to form as followers find potential leaders by passing each other.

Steering behavior: Flocking

Flocking is a steering behavior that combines Separation, Cohesion, and Alignment. Separation behavior avoids other nearby agents. Cohesion behavior keeps the agents in a group. Alignment behavior averages the forward direction by aligning with nearby agents.

What we will do here is replicate the steering behavior, flocking, in blueprint. We will also use UMG to aid the manipulation of weights for each behavior. Let's start now and create the variables we will need in this part of the chapter.

Flocking agents

We must first start off by creating the variables necessary to calculate individual behaviors. Then, we must add the results to normalize a final forward direction for our agent.

Let's focus on our `RollingGameMode` game mode and add the three new global variables we will have to use later in this chapter. In correlation to the three behaviors, we need to create `GlobalAlignment`, `GlobalCohesion`, and `GlobalSeparation` by performing the following steps:

1. Open **RollingGameMode** and focus on EventGraph. Then, from there, create the three variables as a Float type with a default value of 0.0.

    Let's focus back on our **FlockingBall** EventGraph.

2. We need to create three vector variables: **NCohesion**, **NAlignment**, and **NSeperation**.

3. Focus in on the **SphereOverlapActors** node before **ForEachLoop**. Here, we will clear any previous values of the three vectors we just created. We will do this for each of our flocking behaviors, setting it to 0,0,0.

Comment this area **Clear any values**:

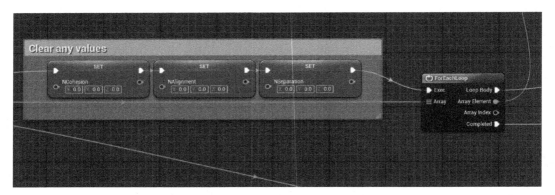

4. Next, before the previously commented part named **Don't follow, followers as the leader**, we want to add space between this and the **Loop Body** pin from the **ForEachLoop** node.

5. First, we need to calculate **NAlignment**, which is the behavior responsible for steering the nearby agents in the same direction. We will get the average direction vector of nearby agents.

6. Now, we want to set a local variable, **NAlignment**, and we will do this by first getting our **Direction** variable from the **Cast to FlockingBall** node. Now, we will need to multiply the **Direction** value by an intensity based on this agent's distance from our agent.

7. We first need to calculate the vector length between us and the agent. We will do this by subtracting our location from the other agent's location. Then, we will get the **VectorLength** value from the results. Next, we will create **Map Range Clamped** and plug in the results from the **VectorLength** node into the **Value** pin.

8. Now, to configure this **Map Range Clamped** node, let's set **In Range B** to **300.0** and then set **Out Range A** to **1.0**. This will result in full intensity when it is at 0 units and there is no intensity beyond 300 units. This return now needs to be multiplied by the **Direction** value.

9. Then, we will add the results of this to **NAlignment** and set this back to the local **NAlignment** variable:

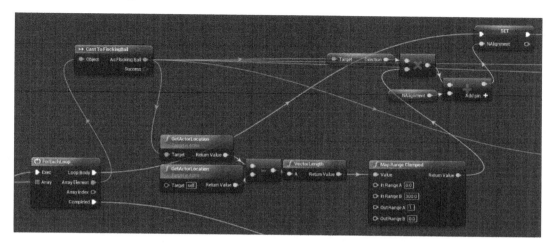

10. Now, we must calculate Cohesion, which is the behavior responsible for steering the agent toward the center of the nearby agents. This is the direction to the agent's center of mass.

11. First, let's create a **GetActorLocation** (A) node and a **Lerp (vector)** node that connects the **A** pin and the **GetActorLocation** (B) node from the reroute. The **Alpha** value should be **Return Value** of **Map Range Clamped** from step 6.

12. Then, we want to add **Return Value** of the **Lerp (vector)** node to **NCohesion**. Next, we will set our local **NCohesion** variable with the final results. This will now update our **NCohesion** variable for each agent nearby:

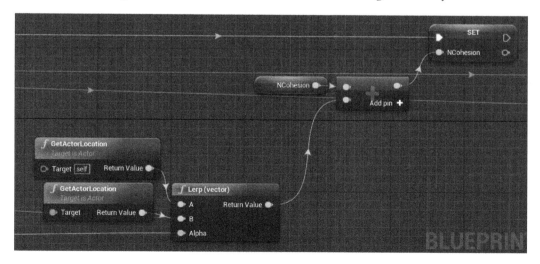

13. The last behavior to calculate is Separation; this is responsible for forcing the agent away from nearby agents. This is the **Direction** vector from our agent to the other agent.

14. We first want to subtract the **GetActorLocation** node from our agent's **GetActorLocation** node. Then, this will be **B** on a **Lerp (vector)** node. We will go back to **Return Value** of the **Map Range Clamped** node and plug this into the **Alpha** pin of the **Lerp (vector)** node. We will leave **A** blank.

15. Then, we must add the **Return Value** of **Lerp (vector)** to **NSeparation**. Lastly, we will set our local **NSeparation** variable with the results.

    Comment this area **Calculate Each Behavior for nearby Agents**:

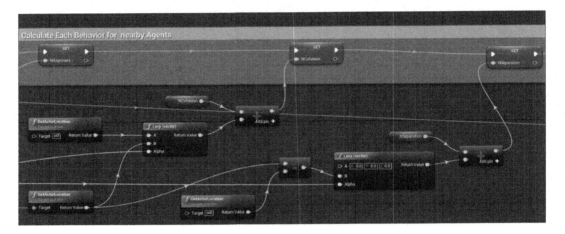

16. Focus in on **Completed** from the **Loop Body** variable.

    Now, we must finish calculating the three behaviors.

17. Let's get the length of the array returned by **SphereOverlapActors** so that we will know how much to divide to create an average. We will then convert this Int to Float. From there, we can divide the **NAlignment** variable and normalize the results using the **Normalize** node. Then, we must get the global variables we defined in RollingGameMode.

18. Create a **Get Game Mode** node and cast it to `RollingGameMode` to get access to our variables. Next, we will get the **Global Alignment** variable from the RollingGameMode casting and multiply it by the **Normalize** results from the previous step. Then, the results of this must be set into the local **NAlignment** variable:

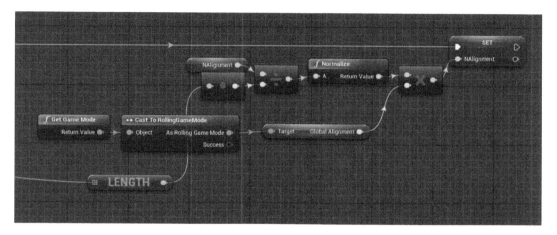

19. Next, we must calculate Cohesion. For this, we must divide the local **NCohesion** variable by the array length and then subtract it from our **GetActorLocation** node. We will then apply the **Normalize** function to gives us the results we need.

20. Next, we will multiply the results by our **Global Cohesion** variable from RollingGameMode. Then, set this to our local **NCohesion** variable:

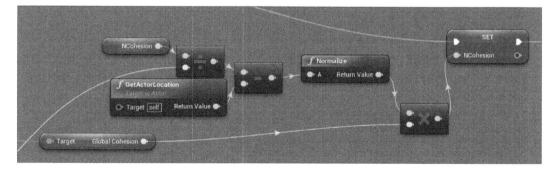

21. Similar to the processes before, we want to get our local **NSeparation** variable and divide it by the array length from before. Mutiply the results by **-1**. Then, multiply the results by the global **Global Separation** variable.

22. Finally, we will get the results and set our local **NSeparation** variable. Comment this area **Calculating Flocking Steering Behavior - outputs NCohession, NAlignment, NSeperation**:

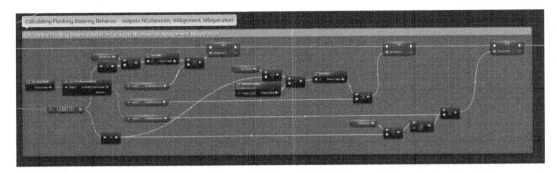

23. Then, we have to find **Calculate Direction** and add each of our variables to the final calculation of the **Direction** variable for this agent:

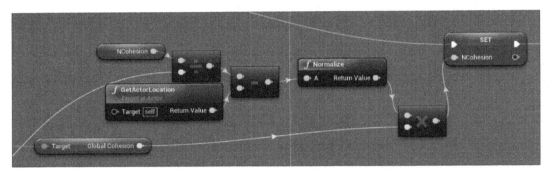

24. The last thing we need to do is prepare for the next section in this course. So, let's find an empty place above **Blueprint** to the left and add some new code.

25. Add a new custom event called **ResetBall**.

26. Next, we want to create a **SetActorLocation** node for this agent and set **New Location** to the **Start Location** variable that we set at the beginning.

27. Now, we want to set a new direction, and we will do this by first placing a **Direction** variable of the **SET** node. Then, we will split the struct and only apply to **Return Value X** and **Return Value Y** from a **Random Unit Vector** node:

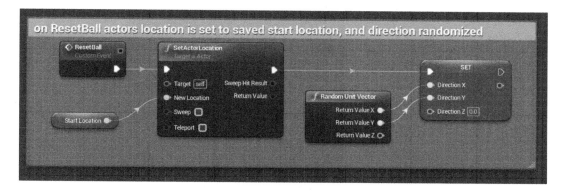

Controlling behavior through UMG

In this part of the chapter, we want to touch on using UMG to control the behaviors influenced upon our agents. We will do this by first creating a UMG widget with the proper controls to manipulate our three float variables. Then, we must assign this user widget to the owning PlayerController. Then, we will end by adding a function that will reset the Agents to their original position, starting the simulation fresh.

A simple UI

Let's navigate to our Content Browser, create a new **Widget** blueprint, and name it FlockingUI. Let's open this up and go to the **Designer** tab to get started, as follows:

1. Let's drag **Vertical Box** into our **Hierarchy** panel.

2. Next, set the slot (**Canvas Panel**) properties: the **Size X** value to **350.0** and the **Size Y** value to **600.0**.

3. Then, drag a button into our **Hierarchy** class under **Vertical Box**. Rename the button **ResetButton**. Next, set the **Vertical Box** slot's **Padding** properties to **75.0** and **25.0**.

4. Lastly, drag **Text** into our **Hierarchy** class under **ResetButton**. Next, set the text property **Text** to "**Reset**":

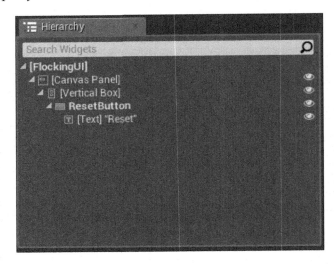

5. Now, let's drag **Horizontal Box** into our **Hierarchy** class under **Vertical Box**. Then, add two more widgets within **Horizontal Box**, which are called **Text** and **Slider**.

6. Now, we must duplicate **Horizontal Box** and its children two more times within the **Hierarchy** class.

7. Right-click and copy **Horizontal Box** and then paste it into **Vertical Box** twice:

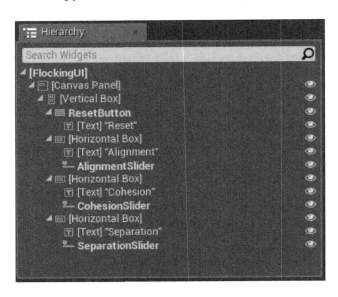

8. After this, we want to rename the widgets we will use for organization purposes. In a sequence, we want to name the first slider **AlignmentSlider**, the second **CohesionSlider**, and the last one **SeparationSlider**.

9. Now, in sequence, let's set our text property **Text** to these three names: **Alignment**, **Cohesion**, and **Separation**. Then, we will set our **Padding** text property to **7.5**.

   Now that this is completed, you should have something similar to the following screenshot:

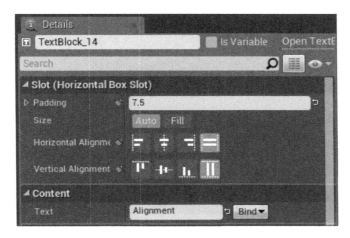

10. To update our **Global** variables, we must create an event from the three sliders. We can start with **AlignmentSlider**, then go under **Events**, and then click on the **+** option on **OnValueChanged**. Then, when this event is called, we will update the **Global Alignment** variable in `RollingGameMode`.

11. Now, we must do this for the other two sliders—**CohesionSlider** and **SeparationSlider**—with the respective global value:

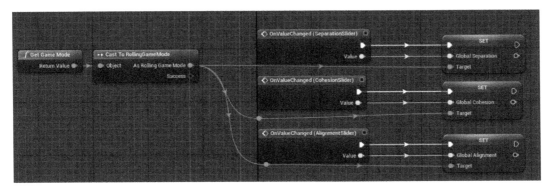

12. Let's focus back on the **Designer** tab of this user widget. Then, click on the **ResetButton** event we made in previous steps.

13. We want to go down in **Events** and click on the **+** option on **OnPressed**. This will give us the event we just created.

14. Here, we want to pull from the pin and call **Get All Actors Of Class**. Next, we want the **Actor Class** value to be **Flocking Ball**. From there, **Out Actors** will return all instances of **Flocking Ball** in the world into an array.

15. The last thing to do is pull from **Out Actors** and call **Reset Ball**. This will notify all our agents to reset the simulation:

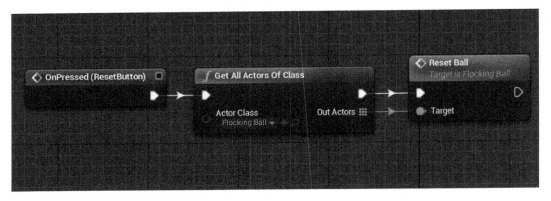

16. Now, we must go back to **Flocking Ball** in EventGraph to add more blueprint code. Find an empty place above the **Reset Ball** event.

17. Right-click and search for **Event Possessed**. Cast a new controller to PlayerController and then pull from **As Player Controller** and search for **Create Widget**. Set the **Class** pin for this node to **FlockingUI**.

18. Next, we must pull from **Return Value** and call **Add to Viewport**. Lastly, we need to show our mouse to the player so that they can interact with the widget.

19. Right-click and search for **Get Player Controller**. Pull from **Return Value** and search for **Show Mouse Cursor**.

Comment this area **Enable Flocking UI & Mouse Visibility**:

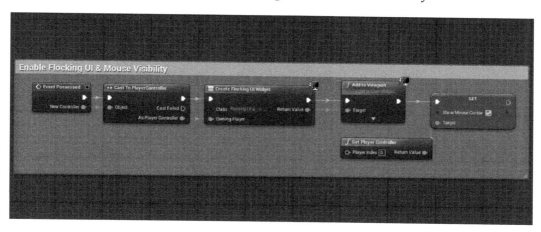

Let's compile everything. Click on **Save All** and go back to our Map. If you hit **Play**, you should see the agents bounce off the walls they collide. Then, if we turn up the different behaviors, we will see that they begin to affect the direction of our agents.

The following screenshot shows what the level looks like after putting everything together:

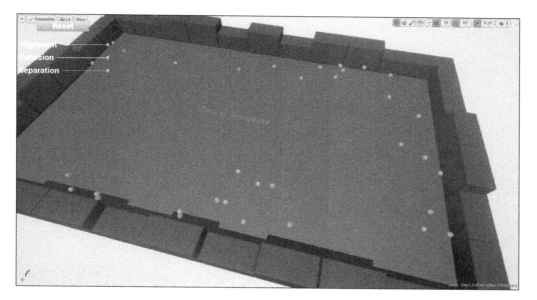

Summary

Let's take some time to briefly talk about what we did in this chapter. First, we set up our agents to bounce off walls. This allows us to watch the agents simulate movement and how the four behaviors would affect them. Next, we will implement the Follower and Leader behavior, and this creates groups within the agents during simulation.

The last thing we did was implement the flocking movement, which is broken up into three different behaviors. The first behavior is Alignment, and it is responsible for aligning agents with nearby agents. The second behavior is Cohesion, and it is responsible for directing agents towards the center of the nearby agents. The third behavior is Separation, and it is responsible for directing the agent away from nearby agents.

Then, we simply created a UI to control the weights we created in the course and reset the agents at any time during the simulation.

Now that we are done covering different movement behaviors, it is time we combined all that we demonstrated about AI in this book. In the next chapter, we will create an AI character, which will patrol, seek, and destroy any enemy. So, let's move on to the next chapter to get started!

8

Creating Patrol, Chase, and Attack AI

In this chapter, we will combine some of the components we used in the previous chapters, including AI Sense and other components, to have AI navigate. Then, we will add some randomness in the time-out time that will make the AI chase after the characters it detects. Now, in this chapter, we can create AI using Behavior Tree while utilizing other AI components. A combination of these components can create responsive and convincing AI behavior.

The goal of this chapter is to create an AI that will fire at you using Behavior Tree; this last AI component will benefit you because there is no perfect solution. So, understanding each of the available tools allows you to exploit the advantages of each component for your use in AI. These tools allow you to create AI that is responsive and convincing.

Creating a Blackboard

Blackboards define the local variable space for Behavior Trees. These Blackboards can also sync with other instances of the same Blackboard. Blackboards can be created first because you'll find yourself modifying them often until you discover everything you need for your Behavior Tree.

We will create our Blackboard data first and then supply it to our Behavior Tree. Now, let's start! Here are the steps:

1. Right-click on the **Content** folder and create a new folder named AI.
2. Now, right-click inside the folder and scroll down to find **Artificial Intelligence**; then, click on **Blackboard**. Let's name this EnemyData.

3. We will open `EnemyData` and then create two object variables to be used by Behavior Tree. Name the first one `TargetActor` and the next one `CurrentRoute`.

 In case you're using Enumeration, you can define the enumeration the same way we will define actors for these objects.

4. Click on **TargetActor** and select the **Key Type** option in the drop-down menu. Then, change the **Base Class** value to **Actor**. We want to do the same with **CurrentRoute**, as in the following screenshot:

Behavior Tree is a tree of nodes whose structural diagram dictates the flow control, each leaf node representing the actual code for the AI to execute. This results in the AI making a sequence of decisions appropriate to the input it receives. To see a sample of what we will end up making today, here is how Behavior Tree looks in Unreal Engine 4:

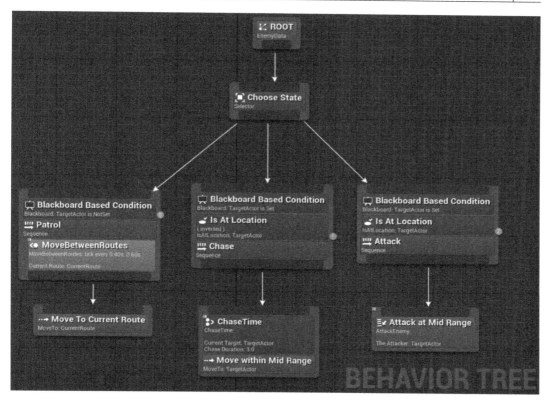

There are many forms of state machines available in the world. Behavior Tree is a form of a tree with a subtree of nodes. It has composites that allow you flow control, resulting in the execution of leaves, which also have additional flow control. This level of control allows you to create deep Behavior Trees with a lot of control.

Let's begin to create our own and get a quick look of what to expect later in the course:

1. We will right-click on **EventGraph** and scroll down to **Artificial Intelligence**. Now, let's click on **Behavior Tree** and name this `EnemyAI`.

2. Open up `EnemyAI`, and you should see **EnemyData** populated in the **ROOT** node. If not, click on the **ROOT** node and set the Blackboard asset to **EnemyData**:

Mid-range attack

This will be a line trace from the center of our eye. This will be how you attack the AI, and this is how the AI will attack you. We will simply run a line trace and then draw a debug line over this, creating a cool red beam out of our player's forehead! We will test to see whether it works, and after this, we will integrate it into both players.

Now, to begin creating this function, we will do something different that will save us time. We will put the function in Blueprint Function Library to be shared across every Blueprint graph.

To keep the function useful for both AIController and PlayerController, we want to to give a controller as the input and then to output an actor. This function will also handle drawing the red beam where necessary:

1. Let's right-click, go to **Blueprints** and then to **Blueprint Function Library**. Name this `EnemyLibrary` and open it up.

2. On the left-hand side, add new **Function**. Name it `LaserFromController`. Make the first input a controller named `theController` and then output an actor named `Hit Actor`. Lastly, create a **Local Variable** called `foundActor`. Make the type **Actor**.

3. Pull from the controller and search for **Get Controlled Pawn**. Then, from here, we will create a line trace based on the character's rotation. Pull from **Get Controlled Pawn** and search for **Get Actor Forward Vector**.

4. We want to multiply **Get Actor Forward Vector** by **9999999**.

5. Go back to **Get Controlled Pawn** from Step 3. Then, cast it to ThirdPersonCharacter, and now we can access the **Mesh** variable. We want the location of our head bone with **Get Socket Location**.

6. Then, pull from **ReturnValue** and find Vector + Vector; now, add **12.0** in the **Z** variable:

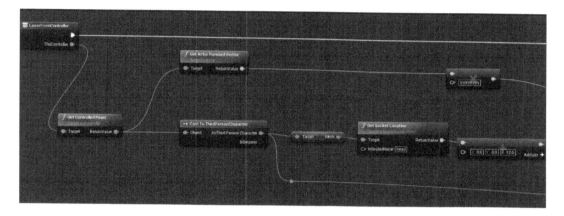

7. Now, we must add the results of Step 4 to the results of Step 6 with a Vector + Vector node. Then, we will move on to a line trace for multiple objects. Search for **LineTraceForObjects** and then plug in the results into the **End** pin of the node we just created.

8. Now, let's set the **Start** value of the node we created in the previous step to the output from the Vector + Vector node to the start. Then, we should have a beam start from his head and draw it forward in space.

9. Pull from **Object Types** and create an array; then, populate the pawn.

10. Pull from **ActorsToIgnore** and create an array; then, populate the **Cast to ThirdPersonCharacter** node into the 0 element.

11. From **LineTraceForObjects**, break **OutHitResult**. Now, pull from **OutHit bBlockingHit** and search for **Branch**.

12. Right-click and search for **Apply Damage**; then, connect the **true** exec pin of the **Branch** node to this node. Pull from **OutHit HitActor** and put it in the **DamagedActor** pin of **Apply Damage**:

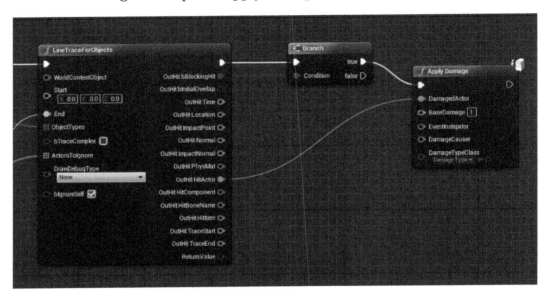

13. Next, right-click and search for **Draw Debug Line**. We want the **LineStart** pin to connect to the results from Step 6, which is the beginning of our line. Then, pull **OutHit Location**, which will be plugged into **LineEnd**. Select the values for **LineColor** as red, for **Duration** as **.2**, and for **Thickness** as **3**.

14. Lastly, pull the local **Found Actor** variable and set it. Pull from **OutHit HitActor** and set it in our local variable. Then, send this to **Return Node**.

15. We want to duplicate **Draw Debug Line** to connect to the **false** exec pin of the **Branch** node:

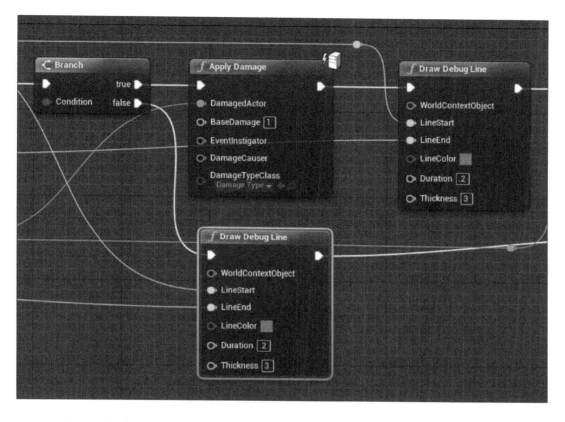

16. Instead of getting **OutHit Location** for **LineEnd**, we will get the results from Step 7.

17. Then, the end of this is plugged into **Return Node**. The **Hit Actor** pin in **Return Node** is populated with our local **Found Actor** variable:

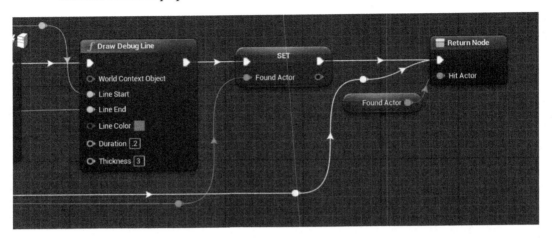

Controllers

In this example, we will give PlayerController the ability to take and apply damage. This is done once the AI is finished, and you'll be able to fight the AI. Also, as we will use AI Perception in this course, we should register the Stimuli source for our controller. Next, we will set up the AIController. We will give it the ability to sense stimuli. Then, we will create an Actor component, which will contain the function needed to update Behavior Tree.

Let's move on and begin to create these base components, as follows:

1. In the **AI** folder, right-click and select **Blueprint**. Then, from the options, select **Player Controller**. Then, we want to name this OutController.

2. Open **Event Graph** and find **Event BeginPlay**.

3. Right-click nearby and search for **Get Controlled Pawn**. Then, pull from **Return Value** and search for **Assign OnTakeAnyDamage**.

4. This will create an **OnTakeAnyDamage** event and output **Damage**.

5. We need to create a variable to hold our **Health** variable. Click on **Add variable** and make a Float variable named **Health**. Set the default to **5**.

6. Looking at **OnTakeAnyDamage**, pull out **Damage** and subtract it from **Health**. Then, set the results in our **Health** variable. Next, we will check whether **Health** is less than or equal to 0.0.

7. Create a **Branch** node from the results. Pull from **True** and right-click to search for **Print String**. Populate this with **Player Died**, right-click, and then search for **DestroyActor**.

8. Right-click and search for **Get Controlled Pawn**; then, plug this into the **Target** pin on **DestroyActor** from the previous step. Now, we can take damage from our AI counterpart:

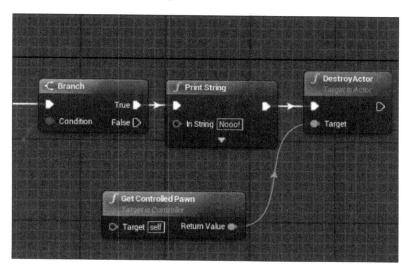

9. Right-click and search for the **E Input** event. Pull **Pressed** and release to search for **Sequence**. Pull from **Then 0** and release to search for **DoOnce**. Pull from **Then 1**, then release to search for **Delay**. Now, set **Duration** to **0.75** and plug **Completed** into the **Reset** pin in **DoOnce**.

10. Looking at **DoOnce**, pull from **Completed**, and release to search for **LaserfromController**. Then, pull from **Hit Actor** and release to search for **Apply Damage**. Set **Duration** to **1.0** and **Damage Causer** to **Self**.

11. Now, we want to add this controller as **StimuliSource**. In the **Components** section, click on **Add Component** and find **AIPerceptionStimuliSource**.

12. Click on **Register** as **Source for Senses** and then click on **+**. Let's select **AISense_Sight** from the available options.

Now, compile this. We are done with our PlayerController setup. Now we need to create an AIController setup so that our AI can fire back at us:

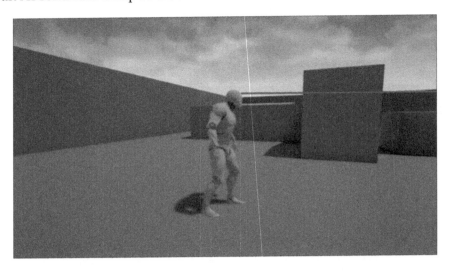

Let's set up our AIController as follows:

1. Right-click and click on **Blueprint**. In all classes, search for **AI Controller**. Select it and then click on **Select** to create it. Name it `EnemyController` and open it in EventGraph.

2. Let's create a new Float variable named **Health**. Then, set the default value to **5.0**.

3. The beginning of this is the same on both characters except for one minor change. So, we can copy the code from `OurController` or start from Step 2 in the previous section. We will copy the section shown in the following screenshot into `EnemyController` from `OurController`:

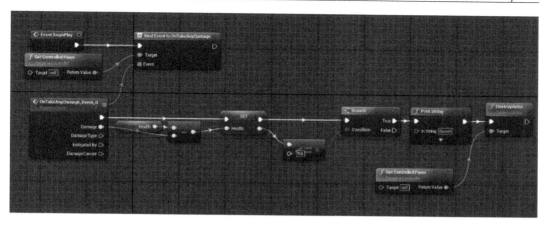

4. At the end of the **Bind Event to OnTakeAnyDamage** event, pull to release and search for **Run Behavior Tree**. Set the **BTAsset** value to **EnemyAI**, which is the asset we created earlier in the chapter. Now, the code in the tree will run on this AIController.

5. Now that the AI can receive damage, we need it to sense the player. We will do this with the AI Perception component.

6. On the **Components** section, click on **Add Component** and search for **AIPerception**. After adding this, under **AI Perception** on the right-hand side, select **Senses Config** from the drop-down menu and hit **+**. Then, set it to **AI Sight config** and select **Sense** from the drop-down menu.

7. Drop down **Detection** by **Affiliation** and check for **Detect Neutrals**.

8. Go under **Events** and click on **OnPerceptionUpdated** to get the currently sensed actors.

9. From **OnPerceptionUpdated (AIPerception)**, pull and release to search for **Sequence**. We want **then_0** to be drawn and then released to search for **DoOnce**. Then, we want **then_1** to be set to the **Duration** pin of the **Delay** node. Set **Duration 1**. Now, connect **Completed** to **Reset**.

10. Focus on **DoOnce**. We will pull from **Completed** and then release to search for **Stop Movement**. Right-click and search for **Blackboard**. Pull from **Blackboard** and release to search for **Set Value as Object**. Right-click, search for **Make Literal Name**, and plug this into **Key Name**. Get the first element from **UpdatedActors** and plug this into **Object Value**:

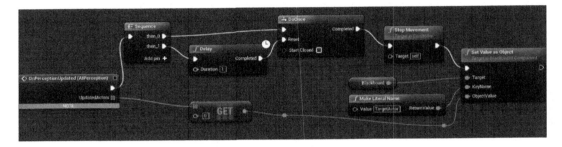

Now, the AI will immediately report the actors that get sensed to Behavior Tree, which then can be used immediately in our AI's next decision.

Waypoints

Similar to the AI Sense project, these waypoints will have a reference to the next waypoint. This simple link between two waypoints allows us to create paths for our AI to navigate to.

Now, we should move on making these waypoints; perform the following steps:

1. To begin, let's right-click in the space inside the **Folder** section and go to **Blueprint**. At the bottom, search in **All Classes** for **TargetPoint**. Select it and then hit **Select** to create it. Then, name it `Waypoint` and open this in EventGraph.

2. On the left-hand side under **My Blueprint**, add a variable waypoint named `NextWaypoint`. We will use this to find the next waypoint to transverse to.

3. Add four waypoints to the level and link them together using the **NextWaypoint** variable. The connection should look similar to A->B->C->D->. D should then connect to A, thus creating a loop.

BT Composites, Task, Decorator, and Service

Tasks are executed by composites. Composites are important because they directly affect the flow control within your Behavior Tree.

Composites come in three forms at the time of writing this: Sequence, Selector, and Simple Parallel. Here's a description of each:

- **Sequence**: This executes each node, returning success on the last node; however, if any node fails, it will immediately return failure and abort the rest of the leaves.

- **Selectors**: This executes each node, returning success immediately and aborting the rest of the leaves. If a node returns failure, it continues to only return failure if the last child returns failure.

- **Simple Parallel**: This executes one task and a subtree at the same time, which allows you to walk and allow another tree of decision making to be at the top of the walk task, for example.

Tasks are usually the last node in the change to be called as they contain the code that would affect the AI actions directly. We will make our own task and learn how it communicates with the Behavior Tree.

Decorators are executed on the entry of a composite or task, which can determine whether the composite or node should be executed. These are great to create custom checks for this specific task. For example, it only executes Break Door if it has the Door and Beast modes.

Services are executed while a subtree is active. This means that it has an available tick. This allows us to gather or update information to make immediate changes in game. The shooting service, for example, would be responsible for shooting whenever the player is in line of sight. This also then allows you to govern the shooting and prevent interruptions when you don't want them.

In this section, we will use everything except Simple Parallel. Let's begin!

First, we will create a Decorator, and it will be responsible for exiting the tree if it goes over the time limit. So, in our case, this will be after 3.0 seconds, and if our move status isn't idle, we will remove **CurrentTarget**, as follows:

1. Right-click on the graph and click on **Blueprint**. Then, go down to **All Classes** and search for **BTD**. Click on **BTDecorator** and then hit **Select** to create a new BT decorator. Name this ChaseTime.

2. Now, let's open **ChaseTime** and go to EventGraph. Right-click and search for **Event Receive Execution Start**.

3. We should create two variables. The first will be a **Blackboard Key Selector** type named CurrentTarget. The second will be a Float type named ChaseDuration.

4. Pull from **Event Receive Execution Start** and then search for **Delay**. Plug in **Chase Duration** into the **Duration** pin of the **Delay** node.

5. Pull from **Owner Actor** and cast this to AIController. Then, get **AsAIController** and search for **Get Move Status**. Pull from **Return Value** and search for **Not Equal To**. Pull from the results and create **Branch**. Plug in **Completed** to the entry of **Branch**.

6. Get **CurrentTarget** and put a variable in EventGraph. Pull from the pin and search for **Set Blackboard Value as Object**. Pull **true** from the **Branch** node into this node. Then, pull from **AsAIController** and search for **Stop Movement**. This should be after **Set Blackboard Value as Object**:

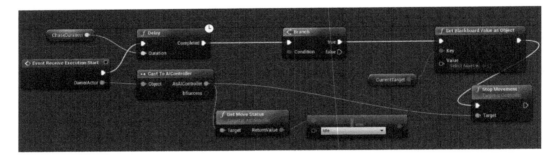

Now that this is done, let's compile it. Then, we will move on to the next component.

Second, we will create a service that will set our first route at random. Then, when we get to the current route, we will move to the next route in the list. This can happen at any moment and services allow you to have a function that can constantly run, as follows:

1. Right-click on the graph and click on **Blueprint**. Then, go down to **All Classes** and then search for **BTS**. Click on **BTService** and hit **Select** to create a new BT service. Name this MoveBetweenRoutes.

2. Open **MoveBetweenRoutes** and navigate to EventGraph.

3. Right-click and search for **Event Receive Activation**. Let's pull from **Owner Actor** and make a pure cast for AIController. Next, pull from **AsAIController** and search for **ReceiveMoveCompleted**. Assign this event for use later:

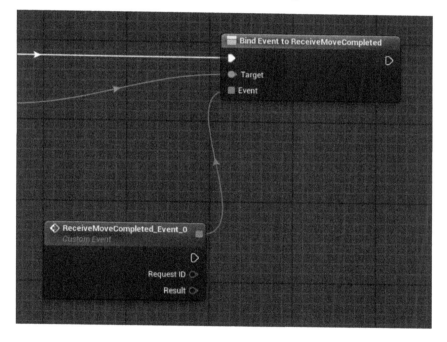

4. Let's create two new variables. The first will be **Blackboard Key Selector** named CurrentRoute. The second will be AIController named thisActor.

5. Now, we want to set **thisActor** and pull **AsAIController** into **thisActor**.

6. Next, we want to get **CurrentRoute** and **Get Blackboard Value as Object**; then, we want to create an **IsValid** node to check whether the Blackboard value object is valid:

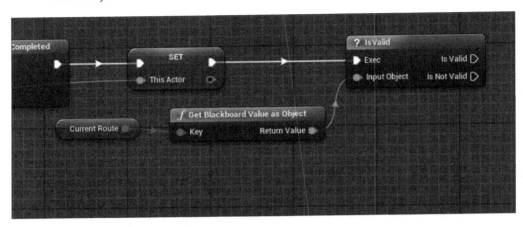

7. Pull from **Is Not Valid** and release to search for **Get All Actors of Class**. Set **Actor Class** to **Waypoint**.

8. Pull from **Out Actors** and release to search for **Length**; then, subtract 1. Right-click and search for **Random Integer in Range**. Then, plug in the results of the minus into **Max**. Next, pull from **Out Actors**, release, and search for **GET**.

9. Plug **Return Value** from **Random Integer in Range** into **Get**. Now, pull down **CurrentRoute**. Pull from this pin, then release, and then search for **Set Blackboard as Object**. Pull **GET** into **Value** of this node:

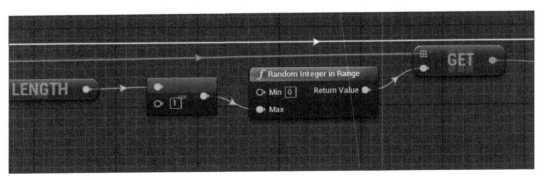

Now, a random route is chosen at the start.

10. Let's focus back on the **ReceiveMoveCompleted** event we created earlier. Switch on **Result**, and from **Success**, release to search for **Branch**.

11. Pull down **thisActor** and then pull pin, then search for **Get Controlled Pawn**. Then, from **ReturnValue**, pull the pin and search for **Get Distance To**.

12. Pull down **CurrentRoute**, pull the pin, and search for **Get Blackboard Value as Object**. Next, cast to waypoint and then plug **AsWaypoint** into **OtherActor**.

13. Check whether **ReturnValue** is less than **125**. Plug the results into **Branch**, which was created earlier:

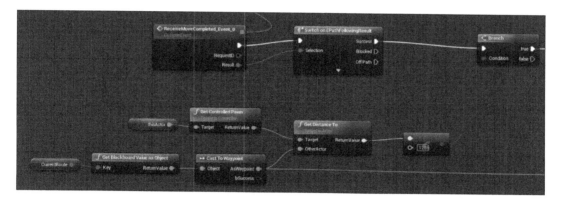

14. Pull from **AsWaypoint** and release to search for **Next Waypoint**.

15. Then, pull down **Current Route** and drop it. Pull the pin and release to search for **Set Blackboard as Object**. Then, pull the pin from **Next Waypoint** into **Value** of this node:

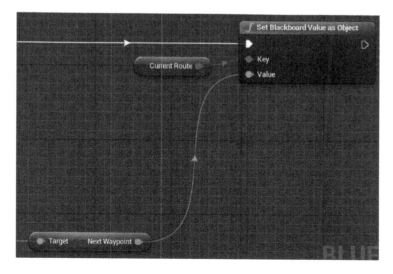

Now, we can move the next route once we've moved close enough to our current route.

The third thing we will create is Task, and it is called as a leaf in the tree. This node will specifically help the AI rotate and attack the player when it's within range. Perform the following steps:

1. Right-click on the graph and click on **Blueprint**. Then, go down to **All Classes** and search for **BTD**. Click on **BTTask** and hit **Select** to create a new **BTTask**. Name this AttackEnemy.

2. Open **AttackEnemy** and then open EventGraph.

3. Right-click and release to search for **Event Receive Execute**. Then, create this node. Now, cast from **Owner Actor** to AIController.

4. From **Cast To AIController**, create a **Branch** node. **False** would go to **Finish Execute**. This will also return **False** for **Success**:

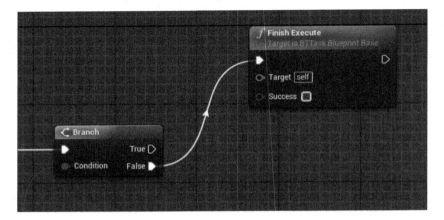

5. Pull down **TheAttacker**, pull the pin, and release to search for **Get Blackboard Value as Object**. Then, we will pull the pin and release to cast to ThirdPersonCharacter. **Success** is then plugged into **Condition** of the **Branch** node we created in Step 4.

6. **True** is then pulled and released to search for **Delay**. In **Duration**, we want to search for **Random Float in Range**. Set the **Min** value to **.4** and the **Max** value to **.75** on the node:

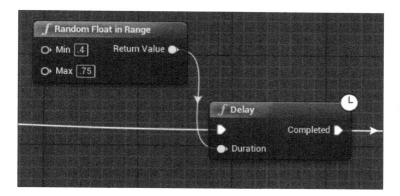

7. Pull from **AsAIController**, release, and then search for **Laser** from **Controller**. Now, pull from **Hit Actor**, release, and search for **Is Valid**. Pull **Is Not Valid** and release to search for **Finish Execute**.

8. Pull from **Is Valid** and search for **Apply Damage**. Then, plug **Hit Actor** into **Damaged Actor**. Plug our **AsAIController** node into **Damage Causer**.

9. Pull from **Apply Damage** and search for **Delay**. Right-click, search for **Random Float in Range**, and then plug **Return Value** into **Duration** of the node we just created. Set the **Min** value to **.5** and the **Max** value to **1.0**.

10. After **Delay**, pull and search for **Finish Execute**. Mark **Success** as true by checking it:

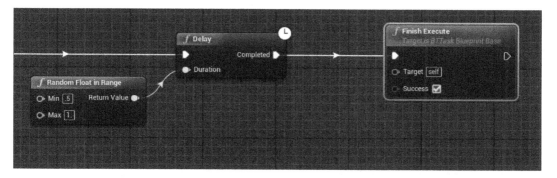

11. Now, right-click on the graph and search for **Event Receive Tick**. Then, cast **Owner Actor** to AIController. From here, we can pull from **AsAIController** and release to search for **Get Controlled Pawn**. Then, pull the **Get Actor Location** pin and release to search for **Get Direction Vector**.

12. Pull from **AsThirdPersonCharacter** to release and search for **GetActorLocation**. Then, plug **ReturnValue** into the **To** pin of **Get Direction Vector**, which was created in the previous step.

13. Pull from **ReturnValue** of **Get Controlled Pawn** and release to search for **Get Actor Forward Vector**. Then, from **ReturnValue**, let's release and search for dot product (.).

14. Plug in **ReturnValue** from the **Get Direction Vector** node into **B**:

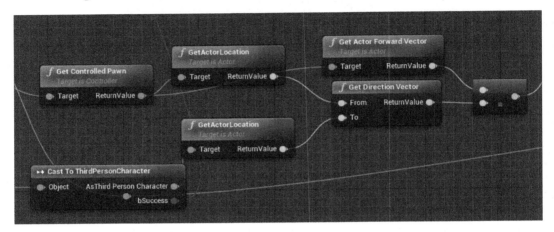

15. Take the results of dot product and release to search for **Radians to Degrees**. Then, pull to release and search for **Absolute**. Lastly, pull results and release to search for **Nearly Equal (float)**. Plug the output from the **Absolute** node into **A**.

16. The **B** value is **57.3**, and the **ErrorTolerance** value is **.1**. This means the range of view is two times the value of **B**. Then, pull **ReturnValue** and release to search for a **Branch** node:

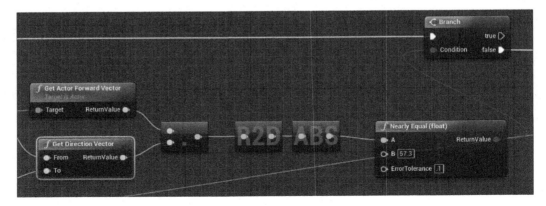

17. Now, pull from **AsAIController** and release after the **Branch** node and then search for **Get Controlled Pawn**. Then, from **Return Value**, pull and release to search for **AddActorWorldRotation**. Right-click and split the struct.

18. From **Return Value** of the **Get Controlled Pawn** node, I will pull and release to search for **GetActorLocation**.

19. Pull down the **The Attacker** variable and release to search for **Get Blackboard Value as Object**, and finally cast it to ThirdPersonCharacter. Then, from **As Third Person Character**, pull the pin and release to search for **GetActorLocation**:

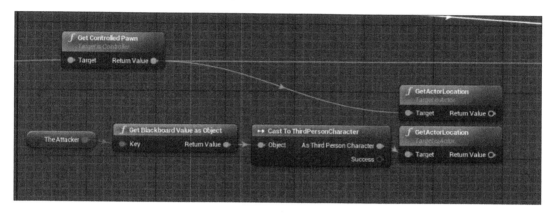

20. Pull from **Return Value** of **Get Controlled Pawn** and plug into **Target** of **GetActorLocation**; then, release to search for **Find Look at Rotation**.

21. Plug in **Return Value** from Step 19 into **Target** of the **Find Look at Rotation** node.

22. Pull from **Get Controlled Pawn** and release to search for **Get Control Rotation**.

23. Pull from **Return Value** of **Find Look at Rotation** and release to search for **Delta (Rotator)**.

24. Plug **Return Value** of **Get Control Rotation** into B of **Delta (Rotator)**:

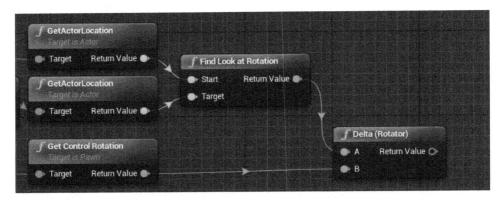

25. Pull from **Return Value** and multiply by the **Get World Delta Seconds** value; further, multiply this by the Float value of **55**. Then, split the rotator and plug in **Z (Yaw)** into **DeltaRotation Z (Yaw)** of the **AddActorWorldRotation** node.

26. Pull from the node and release to search for **Finish Execute**:

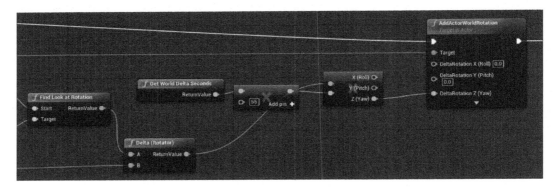

Now that we are done, the AI will rotate toward us whenever we are out of its view.

Creating the logic

Now, we have all our components done. We configured our three custom nodes. Now, we just have to go back to our Behavior Tree. Then, we have to set up three states for the AI to be in. The first is Patrol, which is responsible for moving the AI to the next route. The second is Chase, which is responsible for moving the AI within radius of the player. The final state is Attack, and this state will fire and rotate the AI until Target is no longer within distance.

Now, let's open the `EnemyAI` Behavior Tree via the following steps:

1. Pull down from **Root**, search for **Selector**, and set the **Name to Choose State** node. Here, we will define three distinct states.

2. Pull **Choose State** and search for **Sequence**. Now, right-click, select **Add Decorator**, and find **Blackboard**.

3. Click on **Blackboard** and set **Key Query** to **Is Not Set** and **Blackboard Key** to **TargetActor**.

4. Right-click, click on **Add Service**, and find **MoveBetweenRoutes**.

5. Click on **MoveBetweenRoutes** and set **Current Route** to **CurrentRoute**.

6. Pull from **Sequence** and search for **MoveTo**. Now, set **MoveTo** to **CurrentRoute**:

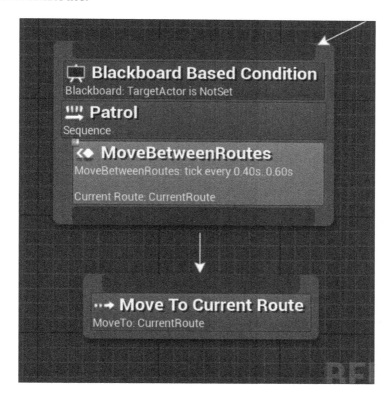

7. Pull **Choose State** and search for **Sequence**. Now, right-click and select **Add Decorator** to find **Blackboard**.

8. Click on **Blackboard** and set **Key Query** to **Is Set** and **Blackboard Key** to **TargetActor**.

9. Right-click and select **Add Decorator**; then, search for **Is At Location**.

10. Click on **Is At Location** and set **Acceptable Radius** to **600.0**, **Inverse Condition** to **True**, and **Blackboard Key** to **TargetActor**. **Inverse Condition** will return **True** if we are outside the **Acceptable Radius** value.

11. Pull from **Sequence** and search for **Move**. Click on **Move** and set **MoveTo** to **TargetActor**.

12. Right-click on the **MoveTo** node, select **Add Decorator**, and search for **ChaseTime**.

13. Click on **ChaseTime** and set **Current Target** to **TargetActor** and **Chase Duration** to **3.0**:

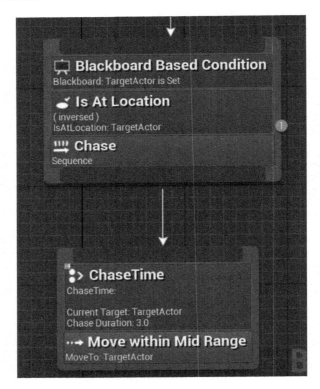

14. Pull from **Choose State** and search for **Sequence**.

15. Right-click, select **Add Decorator**, and search for **Blackboard**. Click on **Blackboard** and set **Key Query** to **Is Set** and **Blackboard Key** to **TargetActor**.

16. Right-click, select **Add Decorator**, and search for **Is At Location**. Click on **Is At Location** and set **Acceptable Radius** to **599.99** and **Blackboard Key** to **TargetActor**.

17. Pull from **Sequence** and search for **Attack at Mid Range**:

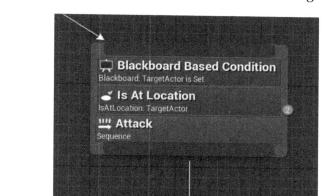

Now, with all these nodes here, you have a complete enemy AI, which you can now fight and take on for yourself! Congratulations on coming this far!

Summary

This chapter contains everything necessary to get started with some impressive AI. We talked about Behavior Trees, which help create decisions for your AI based on situations it encounters. Then, we talked about creating a mid-range attack for you, the player, and the AI to use. We set up the controllers and began setting up the controllers for more functions. The last thing to do before getting everything running in Behavior Tree was to set up the waypoints for the AI to patrol. Finally, we integrated everything into Behavior Tree.

You just learned how to create the basic form of game AI using the tools available within Unreal Engine 4.

We are done! We have created some fun and challenging AI. Let's now get ready for our next chapter. After learning all of this material on AI and Unreal Engine 4 and how they mix together, it is important that we spend a chapter reviewing everything that has been talked about. I will also point out the things we could have done differently. Then, we will be that much closer to a new beginning in the world of game AI!

What Have We Learned?

9

In this chapter, we will briefly glance at some of the chapters. This chapter is important because we will discover the caveats of what we've done. Lastly, we will talk about other examples of what we could achieve with these combined lessons.

In each chapter, the goal was to start with an objective. Then, we approached the objective with a practical demonstration of the knowledge. We talked about what AI means to game AI. We then demonstrated the basics of creating game AI within Unreal Engine 4. What we didn't cover are the issues we may run into. What were the weaknesses and benefits of the techniques we demonstrated? In this chapter, we will answer these questions.

Creating basic AI

There are other forms of AI available. In this book, we created the basic AI. In the hierarchy of the components, there is a controller. The controller then decides which Behavior Tree to run. Then, tasks are chosen based on the sequence of decisions in the tree.

In the controller, we could have an array of different Behavior Trees suited for different tasks. Then, once we approach the task, the tree contains the subtask which aids in coming to a solution. Introducing this level of abstraction requires understanding of which state is necessary to enter.

We demonstrated how to create an AI basic enough to run indefinitely. Using math, we were able to help the AI avoid contacting walls. Presumably, this is all you need for some scenarios. If you need your units to all run independently of each other and avoid the walls as necessary, this script will be perfect for you. However, if you need more control over your units, you can't achieve it with this technique alone.

The alternative is using a control widget, such as a Spline, to control exactly where the AI is going. If you grab the direction to the position on the spline, the AI can be told to move there instead of toward the hero, as we demonstrated in *Chapter 2, Creating Basic AI*.

Here are the pros and cons of using controls to designate where the AI should go.

The pros and cons of using controls

The following is a pro:

- Moving the AI to the exact location

The following are the cons:

- You must create paths by hand
- The paths are limited to control

You can quickly spot the advantages of either use. In a controlled situation, you would use waypoints. These would direct the AI exactly where to move in 3D space. This is perfect to route the AI places in the level you want it to be. So, if it was a Secret Security unit in the game, it would patrol the areas you designate. Then, you can eliminate the player on contact.

Adding randomness and probability

In this chapter, we focused on adapting our previous example to implement randomness and probability. So, we focused on the pros and cons of randomness and probability. Randomness can overlap with probability if you predetermine the outputs. For example, if you want different animations to be played each time a player does a fist attack, you can have an array of different animations you randomly choose from. However, say that there are five available options; with this, you have a 20% chance of choosing any one of the available choices.

The pros and cons of using randomness

The following are the pros:

- There is virtually no limit to the output
- This introduces balance to systems

The following are the cons:

- You must create a large output table for increased deviation
- The paths are limited to control

The pros and cons of using probability

The following are the pros:

- You can predetermine the output
- You can dictate the frequency of output
- You can introduce balance to systems

The following are the cons:

- It is not as random
- You must determine the output table

Probability is powerful when you want to predetermine the output. Probability allows you to choose how often an output is given. Randomness doesn't give you any control on the output. Introducing these can add another layer of abstraction to player experience.

Introducing movement

We only covered movement for pawns because this book is just an introduction. However, if you had any interest in getting other pawn types to move, you have to recreate the junction box, which is the movement component. This movement component for a type of pawn is responsible for taking input delta and converting it into acceleration.

What this means for the car AI is first getting the direction from one point to another, resulting in the position direction. Then, we need to make this position direction relative to the car AI by subtracting it from the car AI's forward direction. This results in a direction delta, which can be applied to the car AI's direction.

You can do something similar in 3D space for a spaceship as well. What this means is that if you want to create a spider AI that can't be moved by the default movement component, then by creating a custom movement component, you can tell the spider AI to move anywhere you wish and still be able to integrate it into the Behavior Tree.

Giving our AI choice

In this chapter, we focused on creating AI with multiple states using Behavior Tree. We also talked briefly about using EQS on the dog to randomly choose an area within its location. This particular example was simple, but when you begin to use filters, the power of EQS shines.

For example, you wanted to get all the enemies within 500 units of your location and eliminate those who aren't within the line of sight. Then, we cleared any enemies not within a 60-degree view angle. Lastly, we got the one closest to the character.

In Blueprint, this can be done, but it then requires you to put it in either Blueprint Library or a node. If we make it in EQS, we are only required to create the conditions in the UI. However, it's easier to share and doesn't require any scripting.

Let's compare using EQS and Blueprint to sense the environment.

The pros and cons of using EQS

The following is a pro:

- No blueprint is required, and it is more intuitive to specify conditions

The following is a con:

- It is limited to the available options in UI

The pros and cons of using Blueprint

The following is a pro:

- There is maximum flexibility for implementation

The following are the cons:

- You must create it from scratch
- It is more difficult to reuse

EQS is a very powerful tool when the purpose of the tool is fully understood. It is capable of quickly and precisely querying a scene without the need to juggle any blueprint code. Paired with blueprint code, you can unlock its true purpose. You can create interfaces, which can be used in the EQS computations, and get the results you want, such as the safest unoccupied place for an AI to run for cover to.

How does our AI sense?

We explained what components to use in order to have our AI sense other pawns in the world. We could customize settings for sight and sound. The perception system would then return any pawn matching these criteria with each update.

We could potentially use the pawns we sense for more than attacking. If we also use it to calculate the best cover, our AI would be reactive to our location. Setting certain criteria allows us to then tell the AI when it's the best time to enter or leave cover. Then, adding additional criteria will allow control over the enter and exit movement behavior.

More advanced movement

Advanced movement allows for flocking behavior. This type of movement behavior is commonly seen by flocks of birds or schools of fish. There is more movement behavior, such as queuing, which tells only one unit to go through a door at a time, for example. Squad behavior is great when you have units that protect each other.

The advantage of using movement behavior is that it doesn't require additional decision making for your AI. This also allows you to take some of the computation out of the tree and calculate it on the pawn.

Creating patrol, chase, and attack AI

We demonstrated how to create AI that will patrol between waypoints you lay within the world. Then, if you ever get in sight of the AI, it will immediately begin to chase you. If you are within the attack range of AI, it will shoot its laser!

I believe each component has its strengths and that they create the most intelligent and responsive AI together. After creating AI without Behavior Tree, you start to wonder whether it's truly necessary to use. The problem dictates the solution, and when you use one solution for every problem, you don't solve anything. I find that using the strengths of Behavior Tree and other components to fill in the weakness results in the most promising behavior.

The pros and cons of using Behavior Tree

The following are the pros:

- It is easily extensible
- It syncs the Blackboard instances

The following are the cons:

- The design dictates the execution flow
- Setup is required

The pros and cons of using blueprint for AI

The following are the pros:

- There is less work for more results
- It doesn't require AIController

The following is a con:

- There is no access to EQS

Using blueprint scripts outside of the tree in order to feed more information to the tree, you can overcome some obstacles of the execution flow within Behavior Trees. For example, if you told the AI to move to a location, you're unable to check for seen enemies during movement unless you use a service. Then, you have to ask whether this service will be useful to this branch specifically or to the tree as a whole.

Summary

I hope I was able to cover everything to get you to confidently start approaching game AI in Unreal Engine 4. Explore the different ideas here and feed your curiosity while exploring game AI. This subject may seem intimidating, but if you've followed everything in this book, you're more than ready to start!

I've had a blast demonstrating the different AI components available in Unreal Engine 4. If you have any questions, feel free to e-mail me at `peterlnewton.com`, and I will get back to you as soon as possible!

Index

Navigation Modifiers 68
Navigation Volumes 13
NavMesh 2, 52
NavMeshModifiers
  about 52
  allowed paths 52
  influence mapping 52
  null paths 52
non-uniform distribution 39
non-uniform distribution, with
      RandomStream 43-45

P

Path Finding 52
Path Following (Path nodes) 3
patrol
  creating 165
pawn detection 103-105
playing 109
probabilistic distribution 38
probability
  about 37, 38
  adding 162
  character, creating with 5
  cons 163
  creating 43
  demonstrating 47
  pros 163
project
  setting up 16, 17

R

randomness
  adding 162
  character, creating with 5
  cons 163
  pros 163
RandomStream 39
realistic movement
  achieving, with Steering 4
RecastNavMesh
  about 55
  example 57, 58
  properties 56, 57
root 6

S

sensory system 3, 11
services 9, 147
simulating 109
state
  resetting 108
state machines 101, 102
state transition 106, 107
state transitions 82-85
Steering
  realistic movement, achieving with 4
steering behaviors 3, 123

T

Target Point 13
tasks 9 147
Third Person template project
  creating 61, 62
tools, Unreal Engine 4
  about 13
  AIController 13
  Behavior Tree 13
  Blackboard Asset 13
  Character 13
  Enumeration 13
  Navigation Component 13
  Navigation Volumes 13
  Target Point 13
tracing 11
transitions
  creating 45, 46

U

UE4 Behavior Tree
  components 6-12
Unreal Engine 4
  tools 13

W

Wander
  adding 40
  project, creating 40-42
waypoints 63, 146

Lightning Source UK Ltd.
Milton Keynes UK
UKOW04f1922100117

291764UK00001B/166/P